Ethical Research with Children

Ethical Research with Children

Ann Farrell

Open University Press

Open University Press
McGraw-Hill Education
McGraw-Hill House
Shoppenhangers Road
Maidenhead, Berkshire
England SL6 2QL

email: enquiries@openup.co.uk
world wide web: www.openup.co.uk

and Two Penn Plaza, New York, NY 1012–2289
USA

First published 2005

A catalogue record of this book is available from the British Library

ISBN-10:   0 335 21650 1 (pb)   0 335 21651 X (hb)
ISBN-13:   9 780 335 216 505 (pb)   9 780 335 216 512 (hb)

Library of Congress Cataloging-in-Publication Data
CIP data has been applied for

Typeset by BookEns Ltd, Royston, Herts.
Printed and bound in Poland by OZGraf. S.A.
www.polskabook.pl

Dedicated to Lindsay and our
children, Anna, Jonathan, David and Julian

Contents

1 Ethics and research with children

Ann Farrell

New times in research ethics are opening up new possibilities for the engagement of children as competent participants in research. These are new times of globalized research productivity, on the one hand, and systematic protective surveillance of children in research, on the other.

This book challenges experienced and emerging practitioner-researchers and research gatekeepers, working in these times, to grapple with the ethical complexities of engaging with children in research.

The term 'ethics' is derived from the Greek *ethos*, meaning character, nature or disposition. The discipline of ethics was evident as early as the Hippocratic school (see Smith 1996). In the eighteenth century the German philosopher Kant wrote of ethics or moral laws as categorical imperatives (see Kant 1995, 2003) and by the nineteenth century authors such as Thomas Percival had begun to translate ethical imperatives into codes of ethics, particularly for medical practice (see Percival 1997; Newsom 1990). Then, in the mid-twentieth century, ethics became an extant field of practice with a reach wider than medical practice and scientific experimentation.

The contemporary field of ethics was born after World War II, largely from worldwide outrage at wartime experimental atrocities. In 1949 the Nuremberg Military Tribunal (NMT) drew ten basic principles for ethical research with humans (Secretariat of the International Military Tribunal 1949). Notably, its moral, ethical and legal obligations covered the voluntary consent of humans to participate in and withdraw from the research without force, deceit or coercion (see also Weithorn and Scherer 1994). The NMT mandated that research contribute to the good of the society and avoid unnecessary physical or mental suffering to participants. Soon thereafter, the World Medical Association (WMA 1954) devised its *Principles for Those in Research and Experimentation* and, in 1964, these principles were adopted as the *Declaration of Helsinki* (see WMA 2000). That same year, the British Medical Research Association published its *Responsibility in Investigations on Human Subjects*, a code of ethical conduct for research supervisors, professional associations and scholarly journals (see also Faden 1986; Coughlin and Beauchamp 1996).

In the1970s, *The Ethics of Drugs Research* was published by the American Academy of Pediatrics (1977) as a set of ethical guidelines for the conduct of biomedical research with children. The decades thereafter saw revisions of the *Helsinki Declaration* by the World Medical Assemblies and, under the auspices of the World Health Organization (WHO) and the Council for International Organizations of Medical Sciences (CIOMS), the *International Ethical Guidelines for Biomedical Research Involving Human Subjects* were published in 1982 and revised in 2002 (see Bankowski 1993). These guidelines focused on scientific validity, risk assessment, consent, individual and community interests and ethical review. McNeill (1993) noted that many countries had adopted a system of ethical review, whereby a research ethics committee would consider whether research proposals met national and international codes of ethics; and eligibility for funding and publication of findings would often be contingent upon compliance with those codes. In due course, ethics review boards were established in countries such as the United Kingdom, the United States, Sweden, Netherlands, Belgium, France, Switzerland, Denmark, Australia and New Zealand (see McNeill 1993; Babbie 1998; Milburn 2001; Miller 2003; Tschudin 2003).

Ethical guidelines for medical research were used as a basis for ethical guidelines for social research. For example, in 1977 the Social Sciences and Humanities Research Council of Canada (SSHRC) published its guidelines on the ethical conduct of social research, and in 1989 Norway established its National Committee for Social Science and Humanities. In due course, Australia's National Health and Medical Research Council extended its guidelines for medical research to cover social and behavioural research (NHMRC 1999), and in 2004 published its *Guidelines for Ethical Conduct in Aboriginal and Torres Strait Island Health Research* (NHMRC 2004).

At the close of the twentieth century, there was an intensified thrust to articulate and embed the principles of ethical research within social science research (Bailey 1978; Kimmel 1988; Burgess 1989; Homan 1991; May 1997; Babbie 1998; Ezzy 2002). There was a parallel thrust in health sciences research (Alderson 1992; Coughlin and Beauchamp 1996; Hoagwood *et al.* 1996; Ross 1998; Fisher *et al.* 2002; Miller 2003; Berg and Latin 2004). Moreover, there was an increasingly sharper focus on ethical research with children (Grodin and Glantz 1994; Hood *et al.* 1996; Mahon *et al.* 1996; Morrow and Richards 1996; Graue *et al.* 1998; Greig and Tayler 1999; Christensen and James 2000).

Ethics and risk

In the new times of globally networked societies, research ethics is being subjected to heightened accountability, regulation and surveillance within what Beck (1992: 1) labels the 'risk society' (see also Castells 1996). A corpus of social theory deals with the regulation of social affairs in risk-producing global societies (Giddens 1991, 2001; Bernstein and Brannen 1996; Lupton 1999; Bessant *et al.* 2003; Kelly 2003). Indeed, risk management, fuelled by a sense of impending peril, has become a prime feature of the new global order. 'Risk now embodies an anxiety that social order and personal well-being alike are under threat' (Bessant *et al.* 2003: 11). Van Swaaningen (1997: 174) argues that the risk society is 'no longer oriented towards positive ideals but towards the negative ideal of limiting risk ... expressed in a negative communality of fear'.

Children, in particular, are being seen to inhabit risky spaces (Danby and Farrell 2004; Farrell 2004); and research with children is being understood as a risky enterprise (Hood *et al.* 1996). The escalating moral panic at the adverse state of society and the attendant risk to children is seen to justify robust measures to heighten protective governance of children and their lives. 'In one crucial sense, the moral panic is the supreme practice of consensual governmentality' (McRobbie 1994: 198; see also Hall *et al.* 1978). So, too, stringent legislation and policy are being designed by adults within a 'principle of "care"' (Jenks 1996: 14) in order to protect children. This thrust is seen in the screening and probity checks of researchers who research with children and young people, for example, in Australia (Danby and Farrell 2004). Protective care is employed because of the perceived danger posed by adults and by dangerous other children (Jenks 1996; Walkerdine 1999). Increasing surveillance of children in research exemplifies the more pervasive regulation of their everyday lives in countries such as the United Kingdom (James and Prout 1997; James and James 1999, 2001) and Australia (Jamrozik and Nocella 1998; Cashmore 2004; Farrell 2001, 2004). The United Nations Convention on the Rights of the Child 1989 (United Nations 1989), the British Children Act 1989 (Her Majesty's Stationery Office (HMSO) 1989) and Protection of Children Act 1999 (HMSO 1999), Queensland's Child Protection Act 1999 (Office of the Queensland Parliamentary Counsel (OQPC) 1999) and its Commission for Children and Young People Act 2000 (OQPC 2000) all exemplify a global concern for child protection.

At the level of research governance, Australia's *National Statement on the Ethical Conduct of Research with Humans* (National Statement), generated federally by the Australian Health Ethics Committee (AHEC/NHMRC 2003), codifies the protective responsibility of researchers engaged in research with children. Such codification is seen also in the codes of ethics/codes of practice of various professional and social research bodies (e.g. the British Educational Research Association, British Psychological Society, British Sociological Association, Australian Association for Research in Education, Australian Psychological Society and American Psychological Association).

Ethical principles in research

Australia's National Statement (NS 1.2–1.5) is typical of many codes of ethics in other developed countries. It identifies the key ethical principles of:

- respect for persons – participants should be treated and protected as autonomous agents (see also Hughes and Helling 1991);
- beneficence – the obligation to maximize possible benefits (and non-maleficence – the obligation to do no harm or to minimize harm) (see also Brock 1994; Fisher *et al.* 1996); and
- justice – addressing who ought to receive the benefits of research and bear its burdens (see also Kimmel 1988).

Rather than seeking to harmonize these principles, the National Statement recognizes the significance of each principle in a particular research context and acknowledges that, in certain circumstances, some principles may be privileged over others (e.g. in some instances, respect for persons may conflict with concern for beneficence). Research ethics, in this respect, is seen to be practical. Singer (1993: 172–3) argues that 'Ethics is practical, or it is not really ethical. We cannot rest content with an ethics that is unsuited to the rough-and-tumble of everyday life'.

Further, various theoretical frameworks have been applied to research ethics. Callahan and Jennings (1983), for example, surveyed a range of frameworks used in social research; while Beauchamp (1996) and Campbell *et al.* (2001) critiqued approaches used in medical research. Espousing a utilitarian framework in social research, authors such as May (1997), Babbie (1998), and Kimmel (1988), argue that ethical research standards are a normative utilitarian set of behaviours, albeit a set that may not always account for escalating social change nor for participants' and researchers' cultural contexts, values and biases (Osuntokun 1993). With respect to research with children, Edwards and Alldred (1999: 266) argue:

> No abstract or universal prescriptive ethical rules can unthinkingly be followed in social research with children, only guidelines for thoughtful considerations within and about the specific contexts … It is not just children and young people's competence to consent that is dependent on context and substance, but that context and substance also inform how they understand the research and make decisions about whether or not to participate.

Ethics has also been theorized as a justificatory discourse concerned with values and value judgments in human affairs (see Preston 1996; Freakley and Burgh 2000). According to Kimmel (1988: 27), for example, ethics is concerned with the distinction between right and wrong or good and evil in relation to the actions, volitions or character of responsible persons, with the term *ethical* connoting rules of behaviour or conformity to a code or set of principles. In his critique of ethical regulation of research ethics in Australia, particularly in humanities research, Cribb (2004: 55) notes that 'ethical behavior springs from a desire to act properly in all circumstances, not just those which have been identified by rule-makers. Ethics exists as a characteristic of humankind precisely because law is inadequate to the task of creating morally good behavior'. Ironically, it can be argued that legislated research ethics has come to surveille and regulate the conduct of research with humans because humans are seen to be at risk of not behaving ethically.

AHEC/NHMRC (2002) acknowledges that, within utilitarian moral approaches, outcomes or consequences of action are the prime criterion upon which to judge the ethical acceptability of research. Thus, actions or policies that promote positive outcomes, understood in terms of improving welfare or satisfaction of preferences, are seen to be ethically acceptable. Conversely, those that are likely to lead to negative consequences, understood in terms of causing harm or frustrating preferences, are seen as less so. Thus, utilitarian moral theories emphasize the 'greatest good for the greatest number' (AHEC/NHMRC 2002).

AHEC also identifies the 'virtue-based approach', pursuing sound moral character traits, such as generosity, goodness, kindness and sympathy (see also Beauchamp 1996). Another approach identified is the 'rights-based approach', focusing on the participant's moral rights such as the right to privacy or to health care. This approach requires assessment of conflicting rights, the propensity for rights violation and a concern to protect rights (see also Alderson 1992). Not surprisingly, a conflict may emerge between utilitarian and rights-based approaches, where the 'greatest good for the greatest number' challenges the primacy of individual rights. Finally, AHEC identifies the approach taken by 'ethical principlism', that is, the application of a set of moral principles to a particular circumstance. A major contributor to the literature around bioethics, this approach draws on a range of moral theories, such as concern with individual rights, respect for persons, the promotion of welfare and avoidance of harm.

Research with children

Our understandings of research with children and, indeed, of ethics in research with children, are embedded within our understandings of children and childhood (see Grodin and Glantz 1994; James *et al.* 1998; James and James 2004). James *et al.* (1988) theorized the history of childhood and distinguished between pre-sociological and sociological versions of childhood. In the nineteenth century, for example, pre-sociological notions of protective kindliness to children and protective reform of childhood were exemplified in the establishment of societies for the prevention of cruelty to both animals and children (see Grodin and Glantz 1994). Then, in the twentieth century, child development, developmental psychology and sociology came to frame much of the theoretical understandings of childhood. Derived from nineteenth-century biology and philosophy, child development, for example, tended to theorize children as 'human becomings' (Phillips and Alderson 2002: 6), that is, as pre-competent people who one day may become adult humans. Developmentalism highlighted the limitations imposed by children's developmental levels and their propensity to impair the quality of research data (see Keith-Spiegel 1983; Touliatos and Compton 1983; Hughes and Helling 1991; Koocher and Keith-Spiegel 1994; Hoagwood et al. 1996; Leikin 1996). Within the developmental frame, the child was seen as an incomplete version of the adult and, by virtue of the child's developmental level, was often short of the requisite capacity, for example, to consent to participation in research (Abramovitch et al. 1991).

In the last decades of the twentieth century, this view of childhood was contested by an alternate view located in the sociology of childhood and new childhood studies (Tobin 1995; Waksler 1996; Corsaro 1997; Danby and Baker 1998; Hutchby and Moran-Ellis 1998; James et al. 1998; Alanen and Mayall 2001; Danby 2002; Mayall 2002, 2003; Danby and Farrell 2004). This sociological view sees children as already competent participants in their everyday worlds (Mackay 1991) and capable of participation in or withdrawal from research. Childhood from this approach, is viewed not as a universal phenomenon, but as socially constructed within specific times, places and contexts, including those that may be constructed as research contexts in which children's active participation is sought and maintained. As Danby and Farrell (2004) argue, this view presents new possibilities for children as competent participants in research.

The book

From these theoretical standpoints, the book covers a range of conceptual, methodological and procedural issues in conducting ethical research with children. In so doing, it provides a framework for practitioner-researchers and research gatekeepers to deal with the ethical aspects of their research with children.

Chapter 2 explores the notions of risk, risk minimization and risk management. Gary Allen critiques the notion of risk culture in light of international trends in the governance and regulation of research ethics within government, higher education and community organizations. A policy corollary identified by Allen is the need for systematic training of researchers and as well as gatekeepers such as research ethics committee members.

Chapter 3 deals with the design of ethical research with children, from initial planning, approval and implementation to dissemination and evaluation. Permeating Priscilla Alderson's chapter is the notion of children as competent research participants. From a children's rights standpoint, Alderson considers ethical and medico-legal understandings of children's consent to participate in research. Alderson argues that research with children requires thoughtful communication, information sharing, and respect and support for children, parents/guardians, researchers and other players within the research.

Chapter 4 explores ethical aspects of research with very young children and those close to them. Lesley Abbott and Ann Langston argue that the very early years present particular challenges to researchers in terms of research scope and methods. Abbott and Langston challenge researchers to determine the fitness of their research methods to the needs, interests and capabilities of very young children in real-world settings.

Chapter 5 identifies the research conversation as a site of research with children, with a particular focus on opening the research conversation. Openings are seen here as sites for the exploration of ethical issues around consent and participation in research. Susan Danby and Ann Farrell show evidence of children engaging in conversations about their experiences of providing informed consent and also present cases where parents override their child's desire to consent to participate in the study, considering these as emblematic of adult governance of children's lives.

Chapter 6 deals with sensitive research, specifically research into child abuse and neglect. Kerryann Walsh presents a focused case of Australian research with early years practitioner-researchers to highlight the challenges of identifying children who may be at risk of or experiencing child abuse and neglect, engaging participants, and dealing with gatekeepers who may be reluctant to disclose possible adverse activities in the research encounter.

Chapter 7 addresses the challenges of conducting research with children and families in Indigenous communities. Drawing on research within First Nations communities in western Canada, Jessica Ball addresses tribal sanction and support of research. Ethical research in these contexts places high priority upon community participation and capacity building through restorative partnerships in order to improve conditions and outcomes for indigenous children and families. While the research example is set in Canada, these issues are increasingly relevant to a wide range of communities beyond Canada that may be characterized by communal rather than individual engagement in research.

Chapter 8 explores crucial issues around inclusion and participation of children with special educational needs and/or disabilities. Monica Cuskelly discusses strategies for negotiating involvement, inclusion and risk minimization for these children. Attention is given to sharing information with children and their families, supporting children throughout the research, and in-service training for practitioners with special needs children.

Chapter 9 examines the ethico-political choices and challenges of transformative research with children. Glenda MacNaughton and Kylie Smith argue that research with children has the capacity to transform relations between the researcher and the researched and that seeking children's voices in research comes with ethico-political decisions about how we act with children once we have heard what they say. They urge researchers to listen to children in ways which can transform their worlds and honour their human rights.

Chapter 10 provides four research stories and the ethical issues the researchers encounter. Tricia David, Jo Tonkin, Sacha Powell and Ceris Anderson craft their research stories into a shared account of the challenges of producing research knowledge within diverse and changing social conditions. They consider the issues faced by the researcher and the researched, particularly with respect to their respective socio-cultural backgrounds, home languages, social mores and power structures.

Chapter 11 focuses on collaborative, transdisciplinary research with children, families and communities and the capacity of research to benefit research participants and the communities in which they live. Collette Tayler, Ann Farrell, Lee Tennent and Carla Patterson consider practical ethics in researching rural communities in Australia within a consortium of government and community agencies. The authors argue that such research needs to provide opportunities for generating trust and mutual respect within and across the research team, the research consortium and the communities in which the research is being conducted.

Chapter 12 is devoted to two research projects conducted with children in England. In a climate of listening to children in research, Virginia Morrow draws lessons from her research in gaining a research sample, participant consent and ongoing participation in research. Morrow locates her cases within the popular constructions of childhood as a period of vulnerability and powerlessness, and juxtaposes these understandings with contemporary sociological understandings of children as competent in research.

Chapter 13 draws together key ideas around the practice of research ethics within the new times of heightened risk and regulation of children's lives. In this chapter Ann Farrell deals with the major challenges of research ethics with children, and then in Chapter 14, she charts a way forward for researchers and research communities who are committed to children being seen and heard in research. The final chapter explores the possibilities for future practitioner research with children that will transform, in positive ways, the lives of children, their families and the societies in which they live.

References

Abramovitch, R., Freedman, J., Thoden K. and Nikolich, C. (1991) Children's capacity to consent to participation in psychological research: Empirical findings, *Child Development*, 62: 1100–9.

Alanen, L. and Mayall, B. (eds) (2001) *Conceptualizing Child–Adult Relations*. London: RoutledgeFalmer.

Alderson, P. (1992) Rights of children and young people, in A. Coote (ed) *The Welfare of Citizens: Developing New Social Rights*. London: Rivers Oram Press.

American Academy of Pediatrics (1997) *The Ethics of Drugs Research*. Elk Grove Village, IL: AAP.

Australian Health Ethics Committee/National Health and Medical Research Council (2002) *Human Research Handbook*. Canberra: AHEC.

Australian Health Ethics Committee/National Health and Medical Research Council (2003) *National Statement on the Ethical Conduct of Research with Humans*. Canberra: AHEC.

Babbie, E. (1998) *The Practice of Social Research*. Belmont, CA: Wadsworth.

Bailey, K.D. (1978) *Methods of Social Research*. New York: Free Press.

Bankowski, Z. (ed.) (1993) *International Ethical Guidelines for Biomedical Research Involving Human Subjects*. Geneva: Council for International Organizations of Medical Sciences.

Beauchamp, T.L. (1996) Moral foundations, In S.S. Coughlin and T. Beauchamp (eds) *Ethics and Epidemiology* (pp. 24–52). New York: Oxford University Press.

Beck, U. (1992) *Risk Society: Towards a New Modernity*. London: Sage.

Berg, K. and Latin, R. (2004) *Essentials of Research Methods in Health, Physical Education, Exercise Science, and Recreation*. Philadelphia: Lippincott Williams and Wilkins.

Bernstein, B. and Brannen, J. (eds) (1996) *Children, Research and Policy*. London: Taylor & Francis.

Bessant, J., Hill, R. and Watts, R. (2003) *Discovering Risk. Social Research and Policy Making*. New York: Peter Lang.

British Medical Research Association (1964) *Responsibility in Investigations on Human Subjects*. London: BMRA.

Brock, D.W. (1994) Ethical issues in exposing children to risks in research, in M.A. Grodin and L.H. Glantz (eds) *Children as Research Subjects: Science, Ethics and Law*, pp. 81–102. New York: Oxford University Press.

Burgess, R.G. (ed.) (1989) *The Ethics of Educational Research*. New York: Falmer Press.

Callahan, D. and Jennings, B. (eds) (1983) *Ethics, the Social Sciences and Policy Analysis*. New York: Plenum Press.

Campbell, A., Gillett, G. and Jones, G. (2001). *Medical Ethics*, 3rd edn. Oxford: Oxford University Press.

Cashmore, J. (2004) Child protection and substitute care: The responsibility of families, community and state, in J.M. Bowes (ed.) *Children, Families and Communities*, 2nd edn, (pp. 169–89). Melbourne: Oxford University Press.

Castells, M. (1996) *The Rise of the Network Society*. Oxford: Blackwell.

Christensen, P. and James, A. (eds) (2000) *Research with Children. Perspectives and Practices*. London: Falmer Press.

Corsaro, W.A. (1997) *The Sociology of Childhood*. Thousand Oaks, CA: Pine Forge Press.

Coughlin, S. and Beauchamp, T. (eds) (1996) *Ethics and Epidemiology*. New York: Oxford University Press.

Council for International Organizations of Medical Sciences (2002) *International Guidelines for Biomedical Research Involving Human Subjects*. Geneva: Council for International Organizations of Medical Sciences.

Cribb, R. (2004) Ethical regulation and humanities research in Australia: Problems and consequences, *Monash Bioethics Review*, 23(3): 39–57.

Danby, S. (2002) The communicative competence of young children, *Australian Journal of Early Childhood*, 27(3): 25–30.

Danby, S. and Baker, C. (1998) 'What's the problem?' – Restoring social order in the preschool classroom, in I. Hutchby and J. Moran-Ellis (eds) *Children and Social Competence: Arenas of Action* (pp. 157–86). London: Falmer Press.

Danby, S. and Farrell, A. (2004) Accounting for young children's competence in education research: New perspectives on research ethics, *Australian Educational Researcher*, 31(3): 35–49.

Edwards, R. and Alldred, P. (1999) Children and young people's views of social research. The case of research on home–school relations, *Childhood*, 6(2): 261–81.

Ezzy, D. (2002) *Qualitative Analysis: Practice and Innovation*. Crows Nest, NSW: Allen & Unwin.

Faden, R. (1986) *A History and Theory of Informed Consent*. Oxford: Oxford University Press.

Farrell, M.A. (2001) Legislative responsibility for child protection and human rights in Queensland, *Australia & New Zealand Journal of Law & Eduction*, 6(1–2): 15–24.

Farrell, A. (2004) Child protection policy perspectives and reform of Australian legislation, *Child Abuse Review*, 13: 234–45.

Fisher, C.B., Hoagwood, K. and Jensen, P.S. (1996) Casebook on ethical issues in research with children and adolescents with mental disorders, in K. Hoagwood, P. Jensen and C.B. Fisher (eds) *Ethical Issues in Mental Health Research with Children and Adolescents* (pp. 135–238). Mahwah, NJ: Lawrence Erlbaum Associates.

Fisher, C., Hoagwo0d, K., Boyce, C. *et al.* (2002) Research ethics for mental health science involving minority children. *American Psychologist,* 57(12): 1024–40.

Freakley, M. and Burgh, G. (2000) *Engaging with Ethics. Ethical Inquiry for Teachers*. Katoomba, NSW: Social Science Press.

Giddens, A. (1991) *Modernity and Self Identity: Self and Society in the Late Modern Age*. Stanford, CA: Stanford University Press.

Giddens, A. (2001) *Sociology*, 4th edn. Cambridge: Polity Press.

Graue, M.E., Walsh, D. and Ceglowski, D. (1998) *Studying Children in Context: Theories, Methods and Ethics*. Thousand Oaks, CA: Sage Publications.

Greig, A. and Tayler, J. (1999) *Doing Research with Children*. London: Sage Publciations.

Grodin, M. and Glantz, L. (eds) (1994) *Children as Research Subjects: Science, Ethics and Law*. New York: Oxford University Press.

Hall, S., Critcher, C. and Jefferson, T. (1978) *Policing the Crisis: Mugging, the State and Law and Order*. London: Macmillan.

Her Majesty's Stationery Office (HMSO) (1989) *Children Act 1989*. London: Queen's Printer of Acts of Parliament.

Her Majesty's Stationery Office (HMSO) (1999) *Protection of Children Act 1999*. London: Queen's Printer of Acts of Parliament.

Hoagwood, K., Jensen, P. and Fisher, C. (eds) (1996) *Ethical Issues in Mental Health Research with Children and Adolescents*. Mahwah, NJ: Lawrence Erlbaum Associates.

Homan, R. (1991) *The Ethics of Social Research*. London: Longman.

Hood, S., Kelly, P. and Mayall, B. (1996) Child as research subjects: a risky enterprise, *Children & Society,* 10(2): 117–28.

Hughes, T. and Helling, M. (1991) A case for obtaining informed consent from young children, *Early Childhood Research Quarterly,* 6: 225–32.

Hutchby, I. and Moran-Ellis, J. (1998) Situating children's social competence, in I. Hutchby and J. Moran-Ellis (eds) *Children and Social Competence: Arenas of Action* (pp. 7–26). London: Falmer Press.

James, A.L. and James, A. (1999) Pump up the volume: Listening to children in separation and divorce, *Childhood,* 6(2): 189–206.

James, A.L. and James, A. (2001) Tightening the net: Children, community and control, *British Journal of Sociology,* 52(2): 211–28.

James, A. and James, A. (2004) *Constructing Childhood. Theory, Policy and Social Practice*. New York: Palgrave Macmillan.

James, A. and Prout, A. (eds) (1997) *Constructing and Reconstructing Childhood*. London: Falmer Press.

James, A., Jenks, C. and Prout, A. (1998) *Theorising Childhood*. Cambridge: Polity Press.

Jamrozik, A. and Nocella, L. (1998) *The Sociology of Social Problems*. Melbourne: Cambridge University Press.

Jenks, C. (1996) *Childhood*. London: Routledge.

Kant, I. (2003) *Critique of Pure Reason* (trans. N. Kemp-Smith). Basingstoke: Palgrave Macmillan. First published in 1781.

Kant, I. (1995) *Foundations of the Metaphysics of Morals and What is Enlightenment* (trans. L.W. Beck). Upper Saddle River, NJ: Prentice Hall. First published in 1785.

Keith-Spiegel, P. (1983) Children and consent to participate in research, in G.B. Melton, G.P. Koocher and M.J. Saks (eds) *Children's Competence to Consent* (pp. 179–211). New York: Plenum.

Kelly, S.E. (2003) Public bioethics and publics: Consensus, boundaries, and participation in biomedical science policy, *Science, Technology & Human Values*, 28: 339–64.

Kimmel, A.J. (1988) *Ethics and Values in Applied Social Research*. Newbury Park, CA: Sage Publications.

Koocher, G.P. and Keith-Spiegel, P. (1994) Scientific issues in psychosocial and educational research with children, in M.A. Grodin and L.H. Glantz (eds) *Children as Research Subjects: Science, Ethics and Law* (pp. 47–80). New York: Oxford University Press.

Leikin, S. (1996) Ethical issues in epidemiologic research with children, in S.S. Coughlin and T. Beauchamp (eds) *Ethics and Epidemiology* (pp. 199–218). New York: Oxford University Press.

Lupton, D. (1999) *Risk*. New York: Routledge.

Mackay, R.W. (1991) Conceptions of children and models of socialization, in F.C. Waksler (ed.) *Studying the Social Worlds of Children: Sociological Readings* (pp. 23–37). London: Falmer Press.

Mahon, A., Glendinning, C., Clarke, K. and Craig, G. (1996) Researching children: Methods and ethics, *Children & Society*, 10(2): 145–54.

May, T. (1997) *Social Research: Issues, Methods and Process*. Buckingham: Open University Press.

Mayall, B. (2002) *Towards Sociology for Childhood: Thinking from Children's Lives*. Buckingham: Open University Press.

Mayall, B. (2003) *Sociologies of Childhood and Educational Thinking*. London: Institute of Education, University of London.

McNeill, P.M. (1993) *The Ethics and Politics of Human Experimentation*. Cambridge: Cambridge University Press.

McRobbie, A. (1994) *Postmodernism and Popular Culture*. London: Routledge.

Milburn, M. (2001) *Informed Choice of Medical Services: Is the Law Just?* Aldershot: Ashgate.

Miller, R.B. (2003) *Children, Ethics and Modern Medicine*. Bloomington: Indiana University Press.

Morrow, V. and Richards, M. (1996) The ethics of social research with children: An overview, *Children & Society*, 10: 90–105.

National Health and Medical Research Council (1999) *National Statement on Ethical Conduct in Research Involving Humans.* http://www.nhmrc.gov.au/issues/human/contents.htm

National Health and Medical Research Council (2004) *National Guidelines for Ethical Conduct in Aboriginal and Torres Strait Island Health Research.* http://www.nhmrc.gov.au/issues/human/contents.htm

Newsom, B. (1990) Medical ethics: Thomas Percival. *JSCV Medical Association*, 86(3): 175.

Office of the Queensland Parliamentary Counsel (1999) *Child Protection Act* (reprint 2A). Brisbane: OQPC (http://www.legislation.qld.gov.au).

Office of the Queensland Parliamentary Counsel (2000) *Commission for Children and Young People Act* (reprint 2E). Brisbane: OQPC (http://www.legislation.qld.gov.au).

Osuntokun, B.O. (1993) Informal consent: a perspective of developing countries, in Z. Bankowski and R.J. Levine (eds) *Ethics and Research on Human Subjects: International Guidelines* (pp. 25–35). Geneva: Council for International Organizations of Medical Sciences.

Percival, T. (1997) *Medical Ethics.* New York: Classics of Surgery Library. First published in 1803.

Phillips, B. and Aldeson, P. (2002) *Beyond 'Anti-Smacking': Challenging Violence and Coercion in Parent–Child Relations.* London: The Children's Society.

Preston, N. (1996) *Understanding Ethics.* Sydney: Federation Press.

Ross, L.F. (1998) *Children, Families and Health Care Decision Making.* Oxford: Clarendon Press.

Secretariat of the International Military Tribunal (1949) *Trials of War Criminals before the Nuremberg Military Tribunals under Control Council Law No. 10*, Vol. 2, pp. 181–2. Washington, DC: US Government Printing Office.

Singer, P. (1993) *Practical Ethics.* Cambridge: Cambridge University Press.

Smith, D.C. (1996) The Hippocratic oath and modern medicine, *Journal of History and Medicine. Allied Sciences,* 51(4): 484–500.

Tobin, J. (1995) Post-structural research in early childhood education, in J. Hatch (ed.) *Qualitative Research in Early Childhood Settings* (pp. 223–43). Westport, CT: Praeger.

Touliatos, J. and Compton, N.H. (1983) *Approaches to Child Study.* Minneapolis, MN: Burgess.

Tschudin, V. (2003) *Ethics in Nursing: The Caring Relationship.* Oxford: Butterworth-Heinemann.

United Nations (1989) *United Nations Convention on the Rights of the Child.* New York: United Nations.

van Swaaningen, R. (1997) *Critical Criminology.* London: Sage.

Walkerdine, V. (1999) Violent girls and precocious girls: Regulating child-hood at the end of the millennium, *Contemporary Issues in Early Childhood,* 1(1): 3–23.

Waksler, F. (1996) *The Little Trials of Childhood and Children's Strategies for Dealing with Them.* London: Falmer Press.

Weithorn, L.A. and Scherer, D.G. (1994) Children's involvement in research participation decisions: Psychological considerations, in M.A. Grodin and L. Glanz (eds) *Children as Research Subjects: Science, Ethics and Law* (pp. 133–79). New York: Oxford University Press.

World Medical Association (1954) *Principles for Those in Research and Experimentation.* Fernay-Voltaire: WMA.

World Medical Association (2000) *Declaration of Helsinki.* Fernay-Voltaire: WMA.

2 Research ethics in a culture of risk
Gary Allen

The governance of human research ethics has been described as an industry (Ashcroft 1999) and, like many industries, the governance of ethical conduct in research is going through a period of rapid change (Kaebnick 2001). For all the regulatory and community interest in this area, there has been little scholarly reflection on the interaction between this burgeoning governance framework and the actual practice and attitudes of researchers across the various disciplines of human research.

The current situation can be summarized as follows:

- Regulators across the developed world have become increasingly interested in the ethical conduct of all human research (rather than just in biomedical research).
- The typical regulatory approach has been to 'stretch' codes and regulations created originally for the biomedical area to cover all research disciplines.
- Institutions are increasingly expected not only to approve proposed human research, but also to monitor its ethical conduct.
- Regulators and funding bodies are holding institutions responsible for any problems with individual projects and are prepared to punish systemic failures.
- The potential consequences of an institution being deemed non-compliant represent a serious risk.
- There is evidence of disquiet amongst some researchers about the typical approaches to the governance of their ethical conduct.
- In an increasingly competitive 'market' where researchers are expected to achieve higher publication rates, successful grant outcomes, and commercialization of their work, researchers still value their academic freedom and professional standing.

Regrettably, for many, 'doing research ethics' has been reduced to a point where it may mean filling out a form and seeking ethical clearance from an ethics committee, rather than a process of reflecting upon the ethical issues in a proposed research design (McNeill 2002: 72).

At the same time, for many institutions, and indeed for many regulators, research ethics has become little more than a cautious process of risk management. As a result, ethics committees can take extremely conservative positions on research proposals, especially when the research design is unfamiliar. The consequence can be the frustration of important and valuable work rather than the protection of vulnerable populations and the facilitation of excellent research (Furedi 2002).

Research ethics should play a positive and important role in the design of research protocols. Research ethics is a fundamental research quality and training issue, but if a research ethics system is to realize its potential, the process cannot be reduced to the act of form-filling or simply risk management. A vital first step in establishing research ethics as a more positive component of the research design process is a clear understanding of the three levels at which the governance of ethical conduct in research operates: at the regulatory, institutional and individual practitioner levels.

Governance and regulation of ethical conduct in human research

Regulatory level

The principles of what it means to conduct human research ethically can be traced back to nineteenth-century philosophy and beyond to the Ancient Greeks (Breen *et al.* 1997). These largely uncodified principles are evident in contemporary codes of ethical conduct for human research. However, it is important to recognize that concepts, such as scientific integrity and minimizing harm, have been very much grounded within the clinical research tradition. And the way in which an issue such as risk is understood, or the way in which risks must be balanced against benefits, draws very much upon the realities of innovative therapeutic practice.

The history of the codified regulation of ethical conduct in human research is far more recent. Internationally, much of what informs our approach to the governance of ethical conduct in human research can be attributed to the *Nuremberg Code* (Secretariat of the International Military Tribunal 1949), the *Declaration of Helsinki* (initially issued in 1964 and updated in 1975, 1983, 1989, 1996, 2000 and 2002; see World Medical Association 2000), and the *Belmont Report* (National Commission for the Protection of Human Subjects of Biomedical and Behavioural Research 1979). These early codes of conduct emerged in response to serious episodes of unethical conduct in medical research (Dodds *et al.* 1994) that resulted in life-threatening harm, and generated significant concern both within and outside the research community. These documents codified the ethical principles of informed consent, integrity, beneficence, respect for persons, and justice. Yet they also were drafted almost exclusively to inform bio-medical practice and were largely silent on the realities and challenges of conducting research in other contexts.

In response to the three early ethical codes, many jurisdictions (e.g. the United Kingdom, the United States, Canada and Australia) established their own human research ethics regimes. These emergent national frameworks established processes for the institutional-level approval and monitoring of human research. Like the international frameworks on which they were based, the various national regimes were (at least initially) focused prima-rily on ethical conduct in clinical research. However, this limited scope has been changing.

In recent decades, these codes of ethics have been evolving, changing from aspirational guidelines written for researchers, to more directive codes of conduct that also articulate institutional responsibilities (see the section on further reading below). These codes are also increasingly being applied outside the biomedical fields to all areas of human research.

What is often forgotten is that, at the same time as these biomedical regimes were emerging, 'codes' of ethical conduct were also appearing for other research disciplines (Breen *et al.* 1997; Ramcharan and Cutcliffe 2001). Though these were generally unwritten principles and structures expressed from within a discipline or professional group (such as market researchers, psychologists, or historians), they represented well-established concepts of what it meant to conduct research ethically in those areas. These 'codes' shared many of the ethical principles informing the biomed-ical codes (Penslar 1995).

Institutional level

In most jurisdictions, the practicalities of the governance of ethical conduct in human research occur at the institutional level. It is the institution that establishes an ethics committee, formulates administrative and policy support for the work of the committee, and (hopefully) resources the com-mittee and encourages a culture of ethical conduct within the institution. As noted, there has been an appreciable shift in the focus of regulators away from informing the practice of individual researchers, and towards articu-lating institutional compliance responsibilities, including a responsibility to train researchers and monitor their conduct.

It is not difficult to find evidence that an institution will be judged harshly for any perceived failure in its governance system (see the further reading section below). Institutional compliance is assessed in terms of all human research within an institution, not just the funded research (i.e. the fact that one project is found to be in breach of ethical standards may result in the suspension of the funding of all research within an institution). Such a suspension can impact upon scores (even hundreds) of researchers and research students, imperil research funding, expose the institution and individuals to civil or criminal proceedings, and significantly harm individual and institutional reputations.

Some of the better-known recent investigations into harm to research participants have focused as much on the operation and effectiveness of the institution's governance framework as on the conduct of the individual protocol. So it should not be surprising that research institutions around the world are increasingly attentive to research ethics as a risk and governance issue.

There is a very real danger that, in the rush to establish rigorous research ethics arrangements that manage an institution's risk exposure, an institution will actually impede research without actually doing anything to promote ethical conduct (Furedi 2002). It is perhaps for this reason that the functioning of ethics committees, particularly in relation to the review of non-medical research, is becoming a more common topic of debate and concern (Ramcharan and Cutcliffe 2001).

Personal level

Even though codes of ethics for human research have existed for many decades, instances of ethical conduct continue to come to light (Thompson 1996). Though perhaps the best-known cases of unethical conduct and harm have related to biomedical research, there have been significant instances of questionable ethical conduct amongst social science researchers (Payne 2000). The potential for harm in social science research has begun to receive media attention and is perhaps one of the drivers for the current regulatory interest in the conduct of researchers outside of the biomedical area (Iphofen 2004).

Despite what has been described as the 'Weberian orthodoxy' where strict regulations are assumed to be the best way of controlling professional conduct, there is some recognition that such directive rules can ignore the importance of an individual's personal commitment to change in their behaviour, the variety of ethical challenges a practitioner can face, or the need for innovative and situational problem-solving (Woodward 1994: 222).

Even though a regulator or professional body may issue a code of ethics for researchers, and an institution may establish local research ethics arrangements, it is researchers who must work out how to apply them. Commentary such as that provided by Saks and Melton (1996) and Misztal (1996) suggests that the degree to which a code of ethics will inform the practice of research is based upon the perceived legitimacy of the issuing agency, the social norms of the group to which the researcher belongs, and the relevance of the content of the code. We ignore this personal level, and the interaction between the three levels, at the peril of creating meaningless bureaucratic structures that will do nothing to address ethical issues in research or to protect institutions from risk.

Understanding the legitimacy gap

Researchers in the non-medical fields may be nervous and suspicious of the current approach to the regulation of ethical conduct, and may consider that the typical ethics committee is ill equipped to review their research (Ramcharan and Cutcliffe 2001; Iphofen 2004). It would appear that many researchers in areas such as the humanities, social sciences and fine arts remain outside of the human research ethics system, even if the relevant national and institutional arrangements indicate that their work is subject to review by an ethics committee. Furthermore, even where such researchers submit their work for review, there is a sense of behavioural compliance, rather than genuine engagement in the process.

From a legitimacy perspective, this is perhaps not surprising. Despite the existence of 'codes' of ethics for many non-medical disciplines, these appear to have largely been ignored in the extension by regulators of biomedical codes to cover all human research. It is true that non-medical scientific academies have often been involved in this process, though the degree to which they have had a genuine opportunity to inform the final code could be questioned (Dodds 2000). There remains a sense that the approach and philosophy of these frameworks are very much grounded within the clinical tradition. Even in the cases where there has been a genuine effort to consult with non-medical researchers (Kondro 1997), national research ethics frameworks have not grown much from their international biomedical roots.

Of course, the suggestion has been made (Rolleston 1997; Dodds 2000) that the core ethical principles of national frameworks, such as the Tri-Council Statement in Canada or the National Statement in Australia, can be applied equally to all human research disciplines, regardless of the apparent clinical focus of those codes. This argument can be accepted, but with qualification. The principles of integrity, respect for persons, beneficence, and justice can be equally applied to all human research (indeed, such principles can be found within many of the 'codes' of ethical conduct for non-medical disciplines). The issue is not whether these ethical principles apply, but it is the manner in which they are described, understood and operationalized. The same standards and solutions used for biomedical research cannot be uniformly applied in a directive fashion to other areas of research. Furthermore, experience from other professional contexts suggests that any attempt to formulate directive rules for application to every contingency is flawed and will ultimately fail (Woodward 1994).

At the institutional level, this situation can place ethics committees in the unenviable position of trying to weigh risks (to potential participants and the institution) without any useful guidance from the regulator. As a consequence, the institution faces the situation of taking conservative positions on any perceived risks, engaging in what might be perceived as arbitrary decision-making, or applying standards that can simply be meaningless to the research practice of the applicants.

An example of the legitimacy gap

The *National Statement on the Ethical Conduct of Research with Humans* (National Statement) (AHEC/NHMRC 2003) is an ethical conduct framework intended for all human research in Australia. The issuing agency, the language used in the code, and the cited sources of the National Statement, all establish that it is the clinical tradition from which the code draws its authority and conceptual origins.

Chapter 4 of the National Statement relates to the participation of children and young people in research. The first ethical principle presented in this chapter is:

> Research is essential to advance knowledge about children's and young peoples' well-being but research involving children and young people ... should only be conducted where ... the research question posed is important to the health and well-being of children or young people. (AHEC/NHMRC 2003)

Clearly, if this ethical principle was applied, literally as stated, research in many disciplinary areas (including education or language studies) should be considered unethical and not be conducted.

This creates a situation where the national code of ethical conduct that must be utilized for all human research fails to provide useful advice to entire disciplinary areas of research. Institutions are also faced with a dilemma of how to manage risk and compliance when the national code is at odds with the realities of their research practice.

Risks in non-clinical research

Just as research, such as educational research, can be a potential source of great benefit to the community (e.g. by informing the development of public policy), it can also be a source of significant harm (SSHRC 2001).

The risks are often very different in non-medical research, and the harms can often be more social than physical, but they are serious nonetheless. These risks can often relate to the presence of unequal power relationships between researchers, third parties and participants (Payne 2000). For example, risks in educational research can include:

- negative impact upon academic results;
- negative impact upon the employability or reputation of educators;
- exposure to criminal, civil or other proceedings;
- negative impact upon peer relationships;
- emotional or psychological distress; and
- negative impact upon familial relationships.

It seems that many researchers feel that ethics committees have treated them and their research unfairly, because of their lack of understanding of their research and a resulting incorrect assessment of the associated risks (Ramcharan and Cutcliffe 2001). By the same token, there is much to suggest that the same researchers are not proficient at recognizing or addressing the risks in their research (Iphofen 2004).

Risks in this context are different from those in biomedical research. Unlike biomedical risk factors, a perceived harm (e.g. a perception that the results of a research project may result in a negative impact upon a young person's grades) can be of just as much concern as an actual harm. Often the complaints about the ethical conduct of such research do not refer to an actual harm, but to the perception that the harm could have occurred. The appropriate remedy for this situation not only requires strategies to address the risks, but also necessitates a researcher providing potential participants with a transparent explanation of the risks and the elements of the research design intended to address those risks.

In practice, solutions to such risks that are based upon the biomedical model are unlikely to be helpful or relevant. In non-clinical research there is no 'medicine bottle' that can be checked for known side effects or contrary indications. Risks in this context tend to be subject to contextual factors and more personal.

Addressing the legitimacy gap

Clearly, the potential impacts of the legitimacy gap are a cause for concern. While it exists, institutions must assess and respond to risk without authoritative guidance, with the very real risk that any decision will be questioned by the regulator and result in punitive action. Similarly, researchers must design and conduct their research without useful guidance on the ethical issues they face, and with no sense of how an ethics committee will assess their work, especially if the research design is innovative or the topic contentious. However, is it unreasonable to expect a single national code to

speak to all disciplinary areas and offer advice on the huge range of different challenges faced by researchers?

Perhaps, rather than institutions looking to the regulator alone to fill
this legitimacy gap, there is a role for an institutional-level framework
where there is a focus upon ensuring that researchers have the 'ethical
tools' to address the challenges they face.

Institutional-level frameworks

Regulators need to engage better with the broad range of scientific and disciplinary bodies. Such an engagement would ensure that national codes can
be perceived as:

- coming from an authoritative source;
- drawing from sources and traditions of broad relevance; and
- using language and examples of broad application.

Nevertheless it would be impossible, and arguably counterproductive, to
attempt to formulate a code that attempts to offer directive principles to
instruct behaviour in every research situation. Instead, we should learn
useful lessons from other professional contexts, such as the public sector,
where a culture of 'ethics learning' is embraced within the institution and
there is a focus upon problem-solving tools and engagement between the
various levels of the process (Longstaff 1994).

In the case of a positive institutional-level human research ethics governance structure, the following features should be present:

- The structure is predicated on facilitating excellent and ethical
  research, and providing guidance and tools that researchers can
  apply to the issues and challenges they face – not attempting to be
  prescriptive or suggesting that there is only one approach to any
  problem.
- The structure is inclusive of different disciplinary and professional
  perspectives (e.g. by including in the membership of the ethics
  committee practitioners from a broad number of disciplinary
  areas).
- The structure offers relevant advice to researchers on the issues
  faced in different areas of research practice (e.g. short and targeted
  discussions on particular issues, such as the conduct of online data
  collection).
- Decision-making (e.g. of the ethics committee) is transparent,
  predictable, timely and based upon accessible standards that
  are subject to review and reflection by the institution's research
  community.

- Research ethics is promoted as a research training and design issue, and is included in the training of students, new researchers and supervisors.
- There is greater engagement between the ethics committee, researchers and administrators, which extends beyond the conduct of information and training sessions, to include ongoing dialogue on the issues really being faced in research practice. This should be a two-way process that informs the development and operation of the institution's research ethics framework.

This kind of approach can increasingly be found within many institutions in Australia, Canada, the United Kingdom and the United States. Those institutions that appear to be 'doing research ethics well' are those that are addressing the relevancy gap with a clear sense of the important interaction between the regulatory, institutional and personal levels, and have established a 'learning institution' approach.

Such a framework requires time, effort and resources. However, the potential rewards for the institution and researchers cannot be overstated. If successfully implemented, an institution's risk exposure can be managed, ethical conduct in research promoted and nurtured, and a far more positive and integrated approach to the governance of research ethics established.

Summary

Research ethics has become an area of significant institutional concern. Unfortunately, the national frameworks against which institutions are judged draw largely upon a clinical model that often has limited relevance to the practice of researchers in other disciplinary areas. As a result, there can often be resistance from researchers to the research ethics process, or at least dissatisfaction with it. This can result in increased risk exposure, potential harm to research participants, or research not being conducted at all. This issue can be addressed by the establishment of institutional-level arrangements that are more relevant to the range of research practice within an institution, and that attempt to assist researchers to find ethically appropriate solutions to the problems they face, rather than mindlessly following directive rules.

Further reading

For discussion on the adequacy of the regulation of ethical conduct in research, and an argument for providing codes of conduct with legislative force, see Gearin (2001), ALRC and AHEC (2001) and Tomossy (2001).

For more about instances of severe punitive action against a research institution, see Russell and Abate (2001), Hotchkin (2001), and Anon. (2000).

For a discussion on the changing nature of codes of ethical conduct of research, from aspirational documents for researchers to more directive documents for institutions, see Dodds (2000).

For commentary on the difficult evolution of the Tri-Council Statement in Canada, and the related consultation process, see Kondro (1997) and Rolleston (1997).

Questions for reflection

1   What risks (whether real, or potentially perceived by your participants or researchers) are present in your own research?
2   Are these risks balanced by the benefits that will flow directly to the participants, or will the risks be justified on the basis of more general benefits?
3   What are some appropriate sources of advice to help you formulate strategies to design your research in such a way as to address these risks?
4   Does the ethical review process in your institution assist you with addressing these risks, and are the kinds of solutions suggested by an ethics committee relevant to your research practice?
5   Has your institution adopted a 'learning institution' approach to the governance of research ethics, rather than the directive application of national standards that might not be relevant to your practice?

References

Anon. (2000) News in brief: Research suspensions, *Monash Bioethics Review*, 19(2): 1 (Ethics Committee Supplement).

Ashcroft, R.E. (1999) The new National Statement on Ethical Conduct in Research Involving Humans: A social theoretic perspective, *Monash Bioethics Review*, 18(4): 14–17 (Ethics Committee Supplement).

Australian Health Ethics Committee/National Health and Medical Research Council (2003) *National Statement on the Ethical Conduct of Research with Humans*. Canberra: AHEC.

Australian Law Reform Commission (ALRC) and Australian Health Ethics Committee (AHEC) (2001) *Protection of Human Genetic Information: Issues Paper*. Canberra: ALRC.

Breen, K., Plueckham, V. and Cordner, S. (1997) *Ethics, Law and Medical Practice*. St Leonards, NSW: Allen & Unwin.

Dodds, S. (2000) Human research ethics in Australia: Ethical regulation and public policy, *Monash Bioethics Review*, 19(2): 4–21 (Ethics Committee Supplement).

Dodds, S., Albury, R. and Thomson, C. (1994) *Ethical Research and Ethics Committee Review of Social and Behavioural Research Proposals: Report to the Department of Human Services and Health*. Canberra: Department of Human Services.

Furedi, F. (2002) Don't rock the research boat, *The Times*, 11 January.

Gearin, M. (2001) Nationwide meetings discuss DNA controls. Australian Broadcasting Corporation TV programme transcript, 17 December. http://www.abc.net.au/7.30/content/2001/s442639.htm (accessed 1 April 2005).

Hotchkin, S. (2001) Johns Hopkins' studies involving human subjects suspended following healthy volunteer's death. *San Francisco Chronicle*, 20 July. http://www.sonoma.edu/users/n/nolan/n400/johnshopkins.htm (accessed 7 March 2002).

Iphofen, R. (2004) A code to keep away judges and MPs, *The Times*, 16 January.

Kaebnick, G.E. (2001) New era(s) in human subject research, *Hastings Center Report*, 31(3): 3.

Kondro, W. (1997) Canada still seeking research code of ethics, *Lancet*, 350(9080): 794.

Longstaff, S. (1994) Why codes fail: and some thoughts about how to make them work!, in N. Preston (ed.) *Ethics for the Public Sector: Education and Training* (pp. 237–46). Leichardt, NSW: Federation Press.

McNeill, P.M. (2002) Research ethics review and the bureaucracy, *Monash Bioethics Review*, 21(3): 72–3.

Misztal, B.A. (1996) *Trust in Modern Societies*. Cambridge: Polity Press.

National Commission for the Protection of Human Subjects of Biomedical and Behavioral Research (1979). The Belmont Report: ethical principles and guidelines for the protection of human subjects of research. *OPRR Reports* 1979; 18 april: 1–8.

Payne, S.L. (2000) Challenges for research ethics and moral knowledge construction in the applied social sciences, *Journal of Business Ethics*, 26(4): 307–18.

Penslar, R. L. (1995) *Research Ethics: Cases and Materials*. Indianapolis: Indiana University Press.

Ramcharan, P. and Cutcliffe, J.R. (2001) Judging the ethics of qualitative research: Considering the 'ethics as process' model, *Health and Social Care in the Community*, 9(6): 358–66.

Rolleston, F. (1997) Developing a Tri-Council code of conduct for research involving humans, *International Journal of Bioethics*, 8(1–2): 67–70.

Russel, S. and Abate, T (2001) Shutdown puts spotlight on human research. Experts say Johns Hopkins case reflects problems across U.S. *San Francisco Chronicle*, 21 July. http://www.sfgate.com/cgi-bin/ article. cgi?file=/chronicle/archive/2001/07/21/MN238758.DTL (accessed 7 March 2002).

Saks, M.J. and Melton, G.B. (1996) Is it possible to legislate morality? Encouraging psychological research contributions to problems of research ethics, in B.H. Stanley, J.E. Sieber and G.B. Melton (eds) *Research Ethics: A Psychological Approach* (pp. 225–53). Lincoln: University of Nebraska Press.

Secretariat of the International Military Tribunal (1949) *Trials of War Criminals before the Nuremburg Military Tribunals under Control Council Law No. 10*, Vol. 2, pp. 181–2. Washington, DC: US Government Printing Office.

Social Sciences and Humanities Research Council. (2001) *Alternative Wor[l]ds: The Humanities in 2010*. Ottawa: SSHRC.

Thompson, W.C. (1996) Research on human judgement and decision making:Implications for informed consent and institutional review, in B.H. Stanley, J.E. Sieber and G.B. Melton (eds) *Research Ethics: A Psychological Approach* (pp. 37–72). Lincoln: University of Nebraska Press.

Tomossy, G. F. (2001) Regulating ethical research: Canadian developments, *Monash Bioethics Review*, 20(4): 67–81.

Woodward, A. (1994) Making ethics part of real work, in N. Preston (ed.) *Ethics for the Public Sector: Education and Training* (pp. 219–36). Leichardt, NSW: Federation Press.

World Medical Association (2000) *Declaration of Helsinki*. Fernay-Voltaire: WMA.

3 Designing ethical research with children
Priscilla Alderson

This chapter reviews ways to design ethical research with children, from the early plans to the final reports and dissemination. It considers the status of children in research design, and their right to be treated as competent research participants in the light of relevant law, guidance and policy, particularly in the United Kingdom and the Commonwealth. Medical ethics concepts of consent and competence are reviewed for their relevance to social research, with the practical concern to promote good standards, rather than merely to avoid poor ones. The two key questions in research design and ways to answer them are reviewed: Is the research worth doing? And is the research explained clearly enough so that anyone asked to take part can make an informed decision about whether they want to consent or refuse? The projects considered include research, consultancies, audit, evaluations and students' case studies.

Research ethics has developed mainly through modern medical ethics. Publicity about Nazi doctors' research made the world aware that research is not part of routine care, and may carry extra risks (Secretariat of the International Military Tribunal 1949). Researchers who are also doctors, teachers, early years staff or students, for example, should, therefore, be clear about when they are either providing services or doing research, and should ask people for their informed, freely given consent before doing research with them (World Medical Association 2000; Australian Health Ethics Committee/National Health and Medical Research Council 2003). While social research often entails only small risks, if any, these may be serious matters to the child concerned. Even asking a simple 'warm-up' question, such as 'Who do you live with?' could make some children feel very pained or embarrassed to talk about their own household. A few guidelines take account of children's own perceptions of risk (Royal College of Paediatrics and Child Health (RCPCH) 2000), besides children's need to know that they can refuse to reply, and that they need not give a reason. Medical ethics tends to be seriously concerned with these issues and can, therefore, set useful standards for social researchers to consider.

Unfortunately, the clear 50-year-old message about the value of consent has not yet been heard and understood universally. Covert research, watching or questioning children without asking their or their parents' permission first, is still widely accepted (British Sociological Association 2003; British Psychological Society 2000). The frequently conducted 'fear of strangers' test with babies involves asking the mother to leave her baby with strangers in a strange room to see how the baby reacts. How many mothers, if they understood the test clearly beforehand and felt able to refuse, would agree to their baby being treated in this way? The following sections outline some basic ideas for designing ethical research.

Three ethical frameworks

Medical ethics draws on three main ethical frameworks:

- The *principles* of respect, justice and doing no harm involve respecting children as sensitive dignified human beings, seeking to be fair, and trying to use resources efficiently.
- *Rights* involve providing for children's basic needs with the best available health care, education and other services that have been developed and tested through research; protecting children from harm, abuse, neglect and discrimination; and promoting children's participation. Participation rights in ethical research include children being well informed, and having their own views listened to and respected by adults (United Nations 1989).
- Best *outcomes* involve strategies for avoiding or reducing harms and costs, and promoting benefits.

These three, and other ethical approaches, are debated for their strengths and shortcomings (Beauchamp and Childress 2001). Moral questions about power, honesty, and respect or abuse may arise throughout the research process. Researchers tend to resolve such questions by thinking about principles (what is the right thing to do), rights (how we can best respect and protect people) or outcomes (what might be the benefits to promote and the harms to avoid). Many researchers combine these approaches, but debate among researchers may arise because different approaches are favoured.

Social research ethics can fill in some gaps in medical ethics (Alderson and Morrow 2004). For example, a serious, though seldom mentioned, ethical problem, is the 'impact on children' of published research reports. If the research questions and methods concentrate on children's needs and failings, so will the reports emphasize problems and deficits. This can increase shame, stigma, prejudice and disadvantage for whole groups of children related to the project, such as all children who are asylum seekers or whose parents are drug addicts. Yet these children may, in some respect, be strong, resilient, knowledgeable and resourceful. Fair, ethical research, therefore, involves asking children about positive as well as well as adverse aspects of their lives, in order to avoid biased reports that may compound their problems. Ethical review and consulting with the children concerned can help researchers to be more aware of 'impact' risks of later reports and help them to plan, early on, how to reduce such later problems.

An example of research that has exploited children's knowledge is the 'Sort it out' survey (Office of Children's Rights Commissioner for London 2001), designed by children and young people and conducted with 3000 young Londoners aged 3–17 years, many of whom were disadvantaged. Their views about the main things that needed improvement in London became the basis for the *State of London's Children* report (Hood 2002) and the Mayor of London's *Strategy for Children and Young People* (Greater London Assembly 2003). Instead of treating problems, such as racism or crime, as children's personal failings, the projects see these as political problems that require political solutions, following the principles of justice, respect and avoiding harm. The programme found, for example, that 43 per cent of London children live in poverty, and that eight major issues for children, including education, health, housing and poverty, cannot be understood in isolation but must be viewed in relation to one another (Hood 2002). This work has set a model for cities across the world to use and to involve children.

Ethics is about helping researchers to become aware of hidden problems and questions in research, and ways of dealing with these, though it does not provide simple answers. Researchers need to know, when they plan their projects, that some journals refuse to publish reports of projects that have not had research ethics committee (REC) approval. Ethical standards change and researchers need to be conversant with them. The safeguards of research ethics, such as applying to an REC for approval, take time but can protect the children who take part in research, and protect researchers from unnecessary criticism or litigation.

Design and the ethical status of children in research

There are three main levels of child involvement in research, as follows:

- Children as *unknowing objects* of research are not asked for their consent and may be unaware that they are being researched.
- Children as *aware subjects* are asked for their informed, willing consent to being observed or questioned, but within fairly rigid adult-designed projects such as questionnaire surveys.

- Children as *active participants* take part willingly in research that has flexible methods: semi-structured interviews with scope for detailed personal accounts, exploring topics through focus groups or drama, diaries, photos or videos, paintings or maps created by the children. Increasingly, children are involved in planning, directing, conducting and/or reporting research projects (Alderson 2000a).

There are advantages when children have greater control as active participants in research. They may enjoy the research process more. The findings may more accurately report their own views and experiences. The risks of their greater participation are that children may confidently contribute and reveal more about themselves, but then later feel greater regret, shame or anger if researchers produce disrespectful or inaccurate reports.

When planning research or reading research reports, it is helpful to picture the model of childhood held by the researcher (Alderson 2000b; Mayall 2002; Alderson and Morrow 2004). A notion of childhood can express the ethical dimensions of the researcher–child relationship, and reveal how the relationship influences the research. Examples include:

- the *innocent child* needing protection;
- the *deprived disadvantaged child* needing resources and services;
- the *criminal child* requiring control;
- the *ignorant child* needing education;
- the *excluded child* who may need special shelter or opportunities;
- the *disabled* child who is the victim of personal tragedy or of a rejecting society; and
- the *strong resourceful child* who can work with adults towards solving problems and creating new opportunities.

Ethical questions

Some researchers see ethics as an afterthought, one last hurdle in planning the project, writing a paragraph for the funders, or getting approval from the REC. Ethics is, however, a vital part of every stage of the project, raising questions and proposing standards, especially about fairly powerless groups such as children. Formal ethics guidelines, such as those articulated by professional associations, can provide useful checklists, but they have gaps, such as usually saying little about children (for example, that of the British Education Research Association 1992). It can be misleading and cause greater problems if researchers follow guidelines with low standards, but believe they are doing 'ethical research', than if they had not thought about ethics at all. Guidelines are useful when they ask hard searching questions about all aspects of research, rather than simply being tick-a-box checklists.

Like the guidelines, RECs can help to raise awareness and standards. Yet there is a risk that, once they have REC approval, researchers may transfer responsibility to the REC. They might say 'This family seems to be very worried and upset by the research, but the REC has approved it, so it must be ethical to go on involving them'. In research teams with strict hierarchies junior researchers who interview children and who find that the children are unhappy about the research, may find it harder to convince their senior colleagues that changes should be made. The director may blame the juniors for being inefficient, or say that the design cannot be changed because it has been approved by the REC, and it is too complicated to reapply to the REC. These kinds of transfer and denial of responsibility undermine ethical standards, which depend on everyone concerned (the whole research team, REC, funder and institution) sharing responsibility to ensure high ethical standards of respect for children and young people.

The value of RECs, and the reason why every project should go through some kind of ethics review, is to remind researchers to think very seriously about two key questions:

- Is the research worth doing?
- Is the research explained clearly enough so that anyone asked to take part can make an informed decision about whether they want to consent or refuse?

The answers to the second question depend on answers to the first, and are dealt with later in this chapter. The first question involves balancing harm and benefit. Researchers often try to balance potential harms, costs and inconvenience, with potential direct benefits to the children taking part in a project. They say that the children may enjoy being interviewed, may learn new skills, gain self-esteem, or benefit from a treatment or package that the research is testing. This is a miscalculation. Research means collecting, analysing and reporting data, and this may not directly benefit children who take part. They might incidentally learn, or enjoy the project, but this cannot be promised, and is not the purpose of the research. Whether they will benefit from a service being tested is often the question for the research and cannot be assured beforehand. The main people to benefit from the research (apart from the researchers) are children in future, when the research findings can show which knowledge and services are useful, or perhaps useless or even harmful.

Therefore, the equation of risk versus hoped-for-but-not-yet-known benefit needs to be balanced between risk to children in the project and possible gain to many children in future, a chalk-and-cheese kind of equation in some ways. This is why it is vital to keep down the risks and costs as much as possible, and not to promise as yet unknown benefits to children and parents in order to persuade them to join a project. Thus, the question 'Is the research worth doing?' becomes 'What benefits do we hope the research will bring to future children and, if these are achieved, do they justify any risks and costs during the project?'. And are these calculations explained clearly enough to children and parents to enable them to decide for themselves if they think the potential benefits are worthwhile. Most projects have several aims and outcomes, and the less practical ones may turn out to be among the most useful to children in the end. For example, a project with children aged 3 years and over who have diabetes made practical recommendations but may be more useful in its new data on young children's early intellectual and moral; which counters many research projects that report young children's supposed ignorance and helpless dependence (Sutcliffe *et al.* 2004).

Ethical questions also arise during the research, and planning ahead can help to avoid or reduce later problems. Here are a few examples:

Funding. Are there any funders who should not be applied to, such as baby milk or arms firms? Might the funders want to alter the research or reports in ways that suit them, or prevent reports from being published if they disagree with the findings? Researchers should make sure from the start that they have a 'freedom to publish' contract.

Research aims. Are there hidden aims, for example, to show that children have extra needs for services that the researchers provide? Is, for instance, child care researched critically from the viewpoint of the children, or only of the parents or the carers? Clearly, the researchers' aims, values and viewpoints shape the findings.

Access. Is the research opt-in, where researchers do not see lists of children's names and addresses? A teacher or nurse may inform the parents/guardians and children, and invite them to contact the researcher only if they wish to know more or to join the project. This takes time and tends to obtain lower response rates, but it does respect participants' privacy and free choice.

Safety. Do researchers have police clearance before contacting children?

Sampling. Are the children selected fairly on grounds of gender, age, ability (including learning and speech), ethnicity, social backgrounds or language (Ward 1997)? Are some children under-involved or over-involved in projects?

Information. Are there simple and clear leaflets that adults can read and explain to very young children or those with learning difficulties? Short words, lines, sentences and paragraphs should be used. Clear use of language is vital. Diagrams and pictures may help. Piloting drafts with children before research sessions (such as interviews) may be advantageous. In Britain RECs require that leaflets explain: the aims, nature and purpose of the research; the main questions; who might benefit from the findings; what participants might gain (if anything); risks or problems; methods, timetable and any activities participants will be asked to take part in; how and where to contact the researchers; and the REC's project number, if there is one. A clear leaflet helps researchers to think clearly about their work (Alderson and Morrow 2004).

Rights. Leaflets can explain that rights include knowing that: you can say 'no' or 'stop' or 'go' or 'pass'; your care (such as education or health) that is related to the research will not change if you refuse to join the project, or if you drop out, and you need not say why you do so; you can choose a research name so that no one else need know what has been told, unless we think someone might be harmed and then we will talk with them about what to do; we will keep the tape and notes locked up so other people cannot see them; we can talk with someone else if you feel upset about the research; you can ask us any questions about the project; we will send you a report at the end of the project.

Consent and competence

Children's consent raises hard, often unresolved, questions. Do we always have to obtain parents' as well as children's consent to research, as most guidance advises? While respecting children's refusal (RCPCH 2000), should we be barred by parents' refusal when children want to join the research? Is a head teacher's permission sufficient, or ought we to ask every child in the school who might be observed? How do we observe whole classes, if one or two children object? How can we reduce the risks of children being coerced into joining a project, but also the equally serious problem of children being unwillingly excluded and silenced? Unhelpful policies and services continue far too long when children are not consulted. One example was the British policy until the 1970s of exporting many children to Australia and Canada without asking for their consent or their evaluations. Many of these questions are still being debated, and one way forward is to discuss them with relevant groups of children, and with adults who support children or who were affected as children themselves in the past, and work towards answers that help them.

Continuing consent during longer projects involves checking that children are still willing to carry on. Sometimes people are afraid to refuse. Researchers need to watch for cues and gently check how participants feel (e.g. during interviews). Anxiety is not necessarily age-related. When interviewing parents in intensive care baby units, I have often kept away from parents who look extra anxious, and this can make projects longer and harder to complete than in a less intensive situation. Valid consent is both informed and willing, when researchers do not exert any 'force, fraud, deceit, duress, over-reaching, or other ulterior form of constraint or coercion' (Secretariat of the International Military Tribunal 1949).

When are children competent enough to consent? This depends on each child's own relevant experience, confidence, the type of research, and the researcher's skill. Standardized tests of competence tend to set unduly high thresholds of competence that many children and some adults fail to reach. Instead, competence to consent to research can be assessed by asking children what they understand about the project and about their rights. This turns into a two-way test, not only of the children but also of the researcher. How well can they inform and listen to the children? Adults must be wary of underestimating children's understanding, and dismissing their refusal as 'stupid or naughty'.

English and much Commonwealth case law is unusual in not having a minimum age of consent to medical treatment. 'Gillick competent' children aged under 16 may give valid consent if they understand the relevant information and can make a wise choice that takes account of their best interests (*Gillick* v. *West Norfolk and Wisbech* AHA [1985] 1 All ER). Some 3- and 4-year-olds with diabetes are able to do this (Sutcliffe *et al.* 2004). Instead of presuming that children are incompetent, researchers could start by assuming that school-age children are competent (RCPCH 2000), because it is easier to prove incompetence than competence. However, although a child's consent to medical treatment may not be overridden by the parents' refusal (*Re W* [1992] 4 All ER 627), lawyers may advise caution in respecting children's refusal, and advise seeking parents' consent to medical research until their children are 18 years old. Social researchers (often reasonably) rely on children's consent without parents' consent. This uncertainty in social research, about when it is reasonable to rely on children's consent alone, needs to be sorted out and formally agreed by RECs rather than by individual researchers in isolation.

Summary

This brief review has raised a few of the many ethical questions that arise in designing research with children. It has given more questions than answers, because ethics helps researchers to be more aware of hidden problems but does not provide easy answers. Ethics guidelines can help us to work towards high standards, rather than simply avoid low ones. The three frameworks of principles, rights and outcomes offer such broad guidance that researchers have to work out how best to apply them in the context of each project. Informing and involving children may block certain research methods, such as covert or deceptive research. Yet new transparent and honest methods and questions may gain more interesting and worthwhile findings about children's own views and values and explanations for their behaviour. This involves respecting children as reasoning, competent participants and finding contemporary participative methods and research designs to fit contemporary ethics.

Questions for reflection

1   How can understanding of principles, rights and outcomes help to raise ethical standards in research with children?
2   How can research ethics committees also help to raise standards?
3   Should social researchers alone be responsible for ethical review of their work?

Further reading

For further discussion on the design of ethical research with children, see Fraser *et al.* (2004). The present chapter summarizes sections from Alderson (2004), which is part of that volume.

References

Alderson, P. (2000a) Children as researchers, in P. Christensen and A. James (eds) *Research with Children* (pp. 241–57). London: RoutledgeFalmer.
Alderson, P. (2000b) *Young Children's Rights*. London: Save the Children/Jessica Kingsley.
Alderson, P. (2004) Ethics, in S. Fraser, V. Lewis, S. Ding, M. Kellett and C. Robinson (eds) *Doing Social Research with Children* (pp. 97–112). London: Sage/Open University.
Alderson, P. and Morrow, G. (2004) *Ethics, Social Research and Consulting with Children and Young People*. Barkingside: Barnardo's.
Australian Health Ethics Committee/National Health and Medical Research Council (2003) *National Statement for the Ethical Conduct of Research Involving Humans*. Canberra: AHEC.

Beauchamp, T. and Childress, J. (2001*) Principles of Biomedical Ethics*. New York: Oxford University Press.

British Education Research Association (1992) *Ethical Guidelines*. Slough: BERA.

British Psychological Society (2000) *A Code of Conduct for Psychologists*. Leicester: BPS.

British Sociological Association (2003) *Statement of Ethical Practice*. Durham: BSA. http://www.britsoc.co.uk (accessed 18 May 2004).

Fraser, S., Lewis, V., Ding, S., Kellett, M. and Robinson, C. (eds) *Doing Social Research with Children*. London: Sage/Open University.

Greater London Assembly (2003) *Mayor's Strategy for Children and Young People*. London: GLA.

Hood, S. (2002) *The State of London's Children*. London: Office of Children's Rights Commissioner for London/National Children's Bureau.

Mayall, B. (2002) *Towards a Sociology for Childhood*. Buckingham: Open University Press.

Office of Children's Rights Commissioner for London (2001) *Sort It Out!* London: OCRCL.

Royal College of Paediatrics and Child Health (2000) Guidelines on the ethical conduct of research with children, *Archives of Disease in Childhood,* 82: 177–82.

Secretariat of thte International Military Tribunal (1949) *Trials of War Criminals before the Nuremberg Military Tribunals under Control Council Law No. 10,* Vol. 2, pp. 1812. Washington, DC: US Government Printing Office.

Sutcliffe, K., Alderson, P. and Curtis, K. (2004) *Children as Partners in Their Diabetes Care*. London: SSRU, Institute of Education.

United Nations (1989) *United Nations Convention on the Rights of the Child*. New York: United Nations.

Ward, L. (1997) *Seen and Heard: Involving Disabled Children and Young People in Research and Development Projects*. York: Joseph Rowntree Foundation.

World Medical Association (2000) *Declaration of Helsinki*. Fernay-Voltaire: WMA.

4 Ethical research with very young children

Lesley Abbott and Ann Langston

This chapter focuses on two studies involving young children and draws on lessons on ethical research learned in these studies. The two studies are: *Birth to Three Matters* (Department for Education and Skills (DfES) 2002), a national study conducted in Britain to identify effective practice with babies and young children in out-of-home settings; and *Educare for the Under Threes* (Abbot and Gillen 1997), another national study focused on the factors affecting the quality of care and education for young children. Throughout the chapter we identify some of the ethical issues which these two studies raise. The age group involved, and to which we refer in this chapter, is from birth to 3 years. We have deliberately not focused on the many and complex areas ably addressed elsewhere in this and other books on research with young children covering issues such as children's rights, their consent to being the focus of research, child protection, health and safety pertaining to their being the subject of photographic and film material. Rather, we provide an honest appraisal of our work, in relation to its intended purpose, its outcomes and the issues we have encountered in presenting it as research. We focus on just two of the many studies of young children and their families in which we have been involved. These have been significant in raising questions about ethical research and what counts as research with very young children.

Our research philosophy

Research with young children is critically important: 'It can advance understanding of how they develop and live their lives, it can contribute to theoretical debates, and its outcomes can impact directly and indirectly on the lives of those researched and others in similar situations' (Lewis 2004: 1). Because it is so powerful, we believe that any research involving very young children must, of necessity, focus on those who live and work in a close relationship with them. Parents, playgroup staff, childminders and childcare workers have a wealth of knowledge about children's capabilities. At the level of observation it can be seen that the dynamics of the relationship between adult and child provide the researcher with unique insights. To isolate the child, as an object of research, from these powerful relationships is only ever to gain a one-dimensional view of them, something we endeavoured to counteract in the projects discussed.

Much of the research in which we have been involved has given prominence to the parent–child dyad, expanding to the parent–child–practitioner triad. Experience has shown that, where research partnerships are based on genuine collaboration between researchers, parents and practitioners, what occurs can be empowering, can benefit partners and can ensure that the research focus is examined from multiple perspectives (Abbott and Gillen 1999).

Research partners, whether practitioners, policy-makers or funding bodies, can influence the nature, form and sometimes the outcomes of the research. An issue in externally funded research is the extent to which funding bodies require or do not require specific outcomes in the form of products or materials, and the way these may subsequently determine the research process. In contrast, a main characteristic of traditional research is that, until the data are gathered and analysed, the product does not unduly govern the nature of the research. In relation to the projects we discuss, in the first the funding body prescribed certain outcomes, while in the second there was no such requirement, thus allowing us the flexibility to work with practitioners and parents to identify a preferred outcome. Some readers of this chapter may then ask whether the first of these projects is indeed true research. In order to elucidate this question we now wish to consider what counts as research.

What do we mean by research?

One of the key questions that arises when working with and finding out about the lives of babies and young children is what constitutes research. Our response would be that neither of the projects under discussion could have been undertaken without research playing a central role in their development. It is important to remind ourselves that academic research was, for many years, the preserve of a predominantly male workforce in universities and laboratories, whilst early childhood research, often conducted by women, is a more recent phenomenon, in its infancy both in terms of the funding it receives and the credibility attached to it. Sylva (1995), for example, in a discussion about the differences between the wide range of research and researchers illustrating the argument above, refers to a 'medieval banquet' attended by 'barons ... from the quantitative alliance ... [men in laboratories?] and troubadours specializing in the rich vein of human discourse known as narrative ... minstrels as well, singing passionately of childhood and its many different voices' [qualitative: women researchers?].

Dichotomies aside, what we pursue in our research is Penn's (1997) notion of 'fitness for purpose', that is, the adoption of research methods that befit the context in which the child spends most of their time in out-of-home time. What seems most important in undertaking research (whether qualitative or quantitative) with very young children and their families, and the practitioners who work with them, is that the methods should be ethical, involve the use of appropriate approaches and fit the purpose in hand, thus ensuring that the picture revealed is as true and accurate as possible.

Evidence from both quantitative and qualitative methods has, however, effectively fulfilled many purposes in relation to both early childhood issues and wider topics (Elfer *et al.* 2002; Evangelou *et al.* 2003), although the products of both methods may be very different, the former frequently presenting reports, statistics and trends, the latter often presenting stories, photographs, film or other descriptions. The product of our research with young children falls into the latter category and the main examples we shall discuss relate to the production of video film and/or books.

As noted, we focus here on two projects, *Birth to Three Matters* and *Educare for the Under Threes*, because they are both studies in which babies and young children were involved.

Birth to Three Matters

The purpose of this study was to identify effective practice with babies and young children in out-of-home settings, a task which could have presented difficulties unless we and the settings in which the study took place had common views of what effective practice looked like in action. In this case there was considerable concord between the two – that is, between us as researchers, and the stakeholders such as managers, parents and practitioners in the many out-of-home settings where we observed practice. Underpinning our own views of what effective practice would look like in action was a vast body of research which both informed and challenged our views of children, their learning, their competence and their infinite capacities.

It is ironic that entry to settings sometimes takes much longer to negotiate than the completion of the research itself, since gaining entry to childcare settings is an increasingly sensitive and complex issue in the United Kingdom, where vetting procedures for those working in and visiting out-of-home settings are very thorough and require criminal records checks to determine the suitability of those involved.

That said, the privilege that comes when one has a long history of training, researching and working with members of the child-care community, meant that for us, engaged on a very welcome and prestigious government-funded project, gaining entry for the purposes of this project was both straightforward and expeditious. It was a favoured position and one which allowed us to avoid the slow and laboured entry to settings we might otherwise have had to pursue. We were able, therefore, with the help of our many colleagues throughout the country, to quickly identify and work with a range of settings where we knew we would locate the sort of practice we think of as 'effective'. So, difficulty in gaining entry to settings was never an issue for us, yet we know that this is frequently the first hurdle where the research process can founder.

In considering the methods we would use to reflect 'effective practice' with children between birth and 3 years of age, we were concerned that the 'medium' adopted must have the power to carry across the message we wished to send. However, we had been asked to produce video material as part of the outcomes for the project so, given these factors, together with the data we had collected on the preferences and dislikes of the target audience and the wider early years community, we decided that our evidence would derive from non-participant observation, using moving pictures (video) and still photography.

Another factor we needed to take account of was time, which was in short supply, since the research had to be completed in less than a year in order to produce a set of materials which were to be printed and distributed immediately after the research phase ended. This being the case, we were not in a position to do more than identify what examples we wished to show as illustrative of effective practice. These included adult–child interaction, the role of a key worker; aspects of children's competence as communicators, learners and individuals; illustrations of children's healthy dependence and independence; examples of children making choices and decisions; and, in relation to adults, the sorts of interactions that would encourage, facilitate and scaffold such behaviours in an environment that supported the child to grow and develop. For this reason we discussed with the camera crew allocated to us by our funding body aspects of practice we wished to capture, and initially agreed to undertake exploratory visits to some of the centres in which we were to film, in order to identify any particular activities or experiences that would support the research focus.

The outcome of the research was a pack of materials containing a video, 16 cards, a CD-ROM, a booklet and a literature review. With the exception of the latter, whose purpose is wider, all other elements illustrate and identify examples of effective practice in work with young children in out-of-home settings. We believe that they provide snapshots of everyday events in the lives of very young children in out-of-home settings.

Reflecting on the issue of entry, since our research was undertaken, has led us to consider whether such privilege is merely advantageous or whether, in our haste to gain immediate access to settings in order to complete the task of producing 'a framework of effective practice', we were breaking the unwritten code of research ethics that ensures, though does not require, that gaining entry is a slow and complicated process. Farrell (2003) notes the requirement in Australia whereby researchers in her institution must adhere by law to the *National Statement on the Ethical Conduct of Research with Humans* (AHEC/NHMRC 2003). Had our access and entry to settings been prescribed in this way it is doubtful whether the project would have started since, as we have indicated, time constraints were a non-negotiable requisite of our funding. However, we were very mindful of ethical issues and, in spite of the fact that had we not been able to deliver the material in time our invitation to undertake this project could easily have been withdrawn, we nevertheless followed the appropriate ethical procedures by gaining permissions and consent from all those concerned.

As highlighted earlier, a further issue was that we had been assigned a camera crew by our funders, which effectively required us to work collaboratively through a third party. We thought that the introduction of the camera crew would allow us to use our time to observe at a distance, discuss with the film director what we wanted to capture and talk to parents and staff about the children and their activities and responses, giving us several perspectives on the same event. This did not happen.

In reality, these factors amalgamated to conspire against us and we found ourselves trying to influence what was to be filmed via a film director with very different views about what the focus of the film should be. Our agreement to specify which aspects of practice and children's experiences in day care we hoped to find led our director to begin to plan ahead, requesting events like 'nappy changing' to take place at a given time in a particular place, rather than waiting for its natural occurrence during the course of the day. We quickly realized that this was not where we wanted to be and we felt we were on a journey which we had not devised. However, as researchers we were conscious that we had to both meet the brief specified by our funding body, whilst remaining true to our beliefs about how research with young children should be conducted. We were adamant that we did not wish to set up situations and determined that what was captured should reflect everyday realities in out-of-home settings.

Our response to the director's attempts to set up situations was to challenge, negotiate, cajole, and at times insist that the film crew should deviate from their literally fixed focus on particular events in order to capture significant events which we identified as unique and momentary, such as the child wallowing in blue paint, the independent 2-year-old sweeping up the sand in readiness for the next child, or the girl catching a bubble as it floated by.

Another pertinent issue that posed problems for us was the impact on child-care settings of the presence at any one time of as many as six or seven large males and their cameras, booms and recording equipment. We witnessed the effects of this presence on babies, practitioners and parents alike, who often found it daunting and intrusive. A feature of this effect was that normally talkative babies and young children, who, influenced by ' "observer effects", that is, the situation being changed as a consequence of the researcher's presence' (Langston *et al.* 2004: 153), were effectively silenced.

On the other hand, the positive outcomes of having a professional film crew at our disposal should not be underestimated. Their presence meant firstly that we were free to truly observe, whereas had we undertaken our own filming we too could have been 'stuck' behind the camera lens, blind to anything occurring beyond its narrow confines. Another plus was that having a number of cameras gave a much broader scope to film multiple events, and later offered other perspectives on the same event, which, in turn, provided a vast amount of data.

A lesson learned from working in this way was not to make assumptions about roles and responsibilities, since we expected, as researchers, that the analysis of the data and the editing and production of the film would be our responsibility. However, the production team assumed that this was part of their brief, and believed that the subsequent production of a film about babies and young children would be unproblematic. Inevitably, the moments we would have selected from the rough edits proved vastly different from theirs, since whilst we, as researchers, and they, as film makers, had seen the same pictures what we saw was through very different eyes – we through the eyes of early years researchers, they through the eyes of film makers. Negotiating and gaining ownership of our material and what would and would not reflect our views of 'effective practice' required sensitivity, tact and understanding on our part.

Educare for the Under Threes

The second study we discuss is *Educare for the Under Threes* (1995–7). This study focused on defining the term 'educare' and identifying factors affecting the quality of care and education for children under 3 years in out-of-home settings. Five researchers, each with a specific research interest, spent a minimum of one day a week each in one of five early childhood settings over a two-year period.

The key areas of focus for the researchers included: adult roles and interactions; definitions of curriculum for children below the age of 3; assessment of very young children; equality of opportunity; and the development of children's self-concept. The five researchers involved in the project represented different research backgrounds and brought with them a range of research experience in child care and early education.

The centres in which the research was conducted were a parent–toddler group; a community nursery; two children's centres and two private day nurseries. Important issues relating to differences began to emerge early in the research, for example, differences between the centres, the researchers and their different research interests.

Gaining access to centres, as we have discussed, is often quite difficult when babies and very young children are involved; those in which rela-tionships are well established and links have already been made are often welcoming and amenable to research being undertaken. The individual researchers who had prior knowledge of or experience in particular centres negotiated entry to them and gained their permission to involve them. Important considerations in choosing a particular centre were that it would be open to scrutiny and that staff and parents would agree to this and be willing to share their practice over an extended period of time. This was considered to be particularly important, since a main feature of the research was that practitioners would become researchers – thus the commitment to such a project would be significant for individual staff and would have implications for the centre/setting as a whole (Edwards 2004), in that they and their practice would inevitably be open to scrutiny whether or not they opted to be directly involved.

A relationship of constant dialogue with practitioners in which their views and those of other involved adults, most especially the children's carers, were sought, was a key focus. The nature of the issues to be explored was discussed in partnership with practitioners and parents who were invited to write up their experiences, concerns, issues and questions for dis-cussion. The range of research techniques employed was also inspired by the partnership ethos. They included: participant and non-participant interviews; semi-structured interviews; questionnaires; case studies; and documentary analysis (e.g. policies and personal writing generated during the project). Observation was at the forefront of our multi-method data col-lection, but we were conscious, even in non-participant observation, of the impact on the settings and individuals involved.

Issues emerging during the research included the researchers':

- different backgrounds, expertise, research involvements, disci-plines and interests;
- knowledge of young children, skill in putting people at their ease, understanding of the issues;
- range of research questions/foci;
- ability to decentre, that is, to look at other issues or not;

- ability to distance themselves when such young children are involved;
- ability to deal with different perceptions/interpretations of a situation when the discipline or focus dominates;
- relationship with parents – degree of success in seeking permission for their child to be involved;
- communication to parents with regard to their understanding of possible long-term effects of such involvement, such as of filming, recording and photographing;
- ability to keep others 'on board';
- awareness of indirect involvement of all staff members; and
- success in gaining permissions on behalf of a child.

A further issue was confidentiality. When working closely with parents, researchers are often told things in confidence, which may be highly relevant to the successful care and education of the child within that setting. Yet, unless parents share concerns directly with staff, or with the child's key worker, the researcher does not have the right to break confidentiality by informing staff, unless about a child protection issue. One might now question whether this is any longer a valid assumption, since the publication of the *Victoria Climbie Inquiry* led by Lord Laming (2003), which suggests that silence is no longer an option and, when in doubt, adults should speak out.

While reflecting the interests of the researchers, the outcomes of the research project were not traditional, since they comprized the basis of a pack of training and support materials for early years workers. Involving practitioners as researchers and encouraging their self-belief and writing skills resulted in the production of two edited books written collaboratively by researchers and practitioners. Two videos were also developed, one introducing the different contexts in which the research was undertaken, and another providing a story of 'life' in the five centres, capturing aspects of the research interests and providing perspectives on the way each centre was addressing these. The production of an activity workbook was designed to offer a means by which practitioners could 'deepen, expand, and challenge current practices and underpinning assumptions' (Abbott 2000: 7), in effect allowing them, we would argue, to draw their own conclusions in respect of the subjects addressed, rather than accepting those offered by us.

Emerging ethical issues

In spite of the intervening years, between the *Educare for the Under Threes* and *Birth to Three Matters*, years during which many developments have taken place in early childhood research, both projects highlight pertinent ethical issues, which we now discuss.

We referred at the start of this chapter to our research philosophy and suggested that each of the projects, whilst different in many respects, gave prominence to partnership, collaboration and communication. The benefits of this approach are that it values the children and those who play a significant role in their lives, as well as providing an opportunity for their voices to be heard, and offers multiple perspectives on the complexities of children's experiences and the practices that influence their care. A less positive outcome of this approach is that research involving large numbers of people inevitably leads to those who do not wish to be involved in the research being drawn into it.

In relation to funded research, we have argued that, on occasions, the funder determines the way in which the research is conducted and may require particular products as an outcome. In the projects under discussion, although both were externally funded, one had specific outcomes laid down, whilst the other gave the researchers more freedom to decide on what the outcomes would be. Interestingly, in spite of these differences the same kinds of products emerged from both – that is, a pack of materials containing a book(let) and video film.

Another issue worthy of discussion is that of the perceived value of one type of research over another. We would argue that written reports containing quantitative information such as that provided in the High Scope Perry Pre-school Study (Schweinhart and Weikart 1993) frequently present valid and significant information and that many research reports are both accessible and powerful in the ways they are presented. However, they may be regarded by some as more valuable than those qualitative reports which tell stories alongside the facts and figures they contain, and, in our view, are frequently the ones that are more accessible.

A further issue is the extent to which the nature of one type of presentation of findings is seen to have greater legitimacy than another. We would contend that, whilst we accept the need for and value of much quantitative research, we believe that it often becomes inaccessible, leaving all but the most interested of amateurs to read a summary of findings, whilst research which is presented in more accessible formats is likely to be explored more fully by the particular audience to whom it is relevant.

This leads to the following questions: 'Who is the research for?' and 'Who would benefit from knowing what it has to say?' or 'Who would take action in response to any messages it conveys?' Clearly, the first of these questions is to some extent governed by responses to the second and third, since purpose and audience are prime factors in any communication. In other words, we would argue that if a particular type of research in early childhood, for example the *Birth to Three Matters* project, is to have an impact on practice, then not only policy-makers but also practitioners should benefit from its findings, since such research is intended for both groups equally, and we believe both would benefit from knowing what it has to say. However, in the case cited, the extent of this impact depended upon the agreement of a government department to fund a large-scale dissemination of research findings and subsequently of local authorities to make an impact on practice, through both policy decisions and training programmes. An example of the way in which quantitative and qualitative findings have been interwoven is in the Effective Provision of Pre-school Education study (Sylva *et al.* 2003) where case studies are included alongside statistical evidence, making findings more accessible to a wider audience, in particular early childhood practitioners.

The issue of which groups might take action in response to any message research conveys is a bigger question since action needed may clearly be both strategic and economic, and policy development may be a requisite of responsiveness. This is the case in, for example, debates about the need for mass vaccination of infants and screening pregnant mothers for genetic abnormalities in their unborn children. In cases involving decisions about allocation of funding, for example in the case of an increase in the provision of pre-school education, the funders, in this case the Treasury, will demand evidence of the benefits of investment. This is demonstrated by the requirements of the National Evaluation of Early Excellence Centres (Pilot Program) (Bertram and Pascal 2000), in which outcomes similar to those identified in the High Scope Perry Pre-School Study (Schweinhart and Weikart 1993) were expected.

Summary

The two research projects discussed here had very different starting points, which resulted in the production of a range of materials which can be used and interpreted in different ways and at different levels. We are aware that the outcomes of our research are untraditional, but we believe that our methodologies allow for a more individual interpretation of data and presentation of findings, giving us the confidence to claim that our work is 'real research' from the 'qualitative alliance' made accessible both in the way it is presented and through the stories it tells of children in day care in England. Our hope is that those who work and research with babies and young children in day care will feel motivated to engage with it because of both the messages it conveys and the medium through which it is presented.

Questions for reflection

1   Consider the value for children, practitioners, parents and researchers of collaborative research undertaken in early childhood settings. Discuss the costs and benefits of this approach to research.
2   What are the challenges of practitioner-based and academic research in early childhood settings?

Further reading

For a discussion on research in early childhood, see Langston *et al.* (2004). For further insight on researching from children's perspectives, see Lewis and Lindsay (1999).

References

Abbott, L. and Gillen, J. (eds) (1997) *Educare for the Under Threes. Identifying Need and Opportunity*. Manchester: Manchester Metropolitan University.

Abbott, L. and Gillen, J. (1999) Revelations through research partnerships, *Early Years*, 20(1): 43–51.

Australian Health Ethics Committee National Health and Medical Research Council (NHMRC) (2003) *National Statement on the Ethical Conduct of Research Involving Humans*. http://www.nhmrc.gov.au/issues/human/contents.htm

Bertram, T. and Pascal, C. (2000) *Early Excellence Centres Pilot Programme Annual Evaluation Report*. Worcester: Worcester University College.

Department for Educaction and Skills (2002) *Birth to Three Matters*. London: DfES Publications.

Edwards, A. (2004) Education, in S. Fraser, V. Lewis, S. Ding, M. Kellett and C. Robinson (eds) *Doing Research with Young Children*. London: Sage Publications in association with the Open University.

Elfer, P., Goldschied, E. and Selleck, D. (2002) *Key Persons in Nurseries: Building Relationships for Quality Provision*. London: NEYN.

Evangelou, M., Pring, R. and Sylva, K. (2003) *Birth to School Study, Peers Early Education Partnership* (PEEP). Evaluation Short Progress Report submitted to DfES, September.

Farrell, A. (2003) Researching with children: Ethics and expediency. Paper presented to Manchester Metropolitan University research seminar, October.

Langston, A., Abbott, L., Lewis, V., and Kellett, M. (2004) Early childhood, in S. Fraser, V. Lewis, S. Ding, M. Kellett and C. Robinson (eds) *Doing Research with Young Children*. London: Sage Publications in association with the Open University.

Lewis, V. (2004) Diong research with young children, in S. Fraser, V. Lewis, S. Ding, M. Kellett and C. Robinson (eds) *Doing Research with Young Children*. London: Sage/Open University.

Lewis, A. and Lindsay, G. (eds) (1999) *Researching Children's Perspectives*. Buckingham: Open University Press.

Laming, H. (2003) *The Victoria Climbié Inquiry. Report of an Inquiry*, Cm. 5730. Norwich: HMSO.

Penn, H. (1997) *Transforming Nursery Education*. London: Paul Chapman Publishing.

Schweinhart, L.J. and Weikart, D.P. (1993) *A Summary of Significant Benefits: The High Scope Perry Pre-School Study through Age 27*. London: High Scope UK.

Sylva, K. (1995) Research as a medieval banquet – barons, troubadours and minstrels. Paper presented at the RSA Start Right Conference, London, September.

Sylva, K., Melhuish, E., Sammons, P., Siraj-Blatchford, I., Taggart, B. and Elliot, K. (2003) *The Effective Provision of Pre-School Education Project: Findings from the Pre-school Period. Summary of Findings*. London: Institute of Education, University of London.

5 Opening the research conversation

Susan Danby and Ann Farrell

Much contemporary research with children claims to use the research conversation to listen to children on issues that affect them. The notion that children are capable of consulting with adults in the research conversation has come to underpin policy reform agendas in child and family services in both Australia (AHRC/ALRC 1997,; MacNaughton *et al.* 2004; Tayler *et al.* 2004) and the United Kingdom (Clarke *et al.* 2003; Edwards and Alldred 1999; Malone 2003; Stafford *et al.* 2003). Underlying this consultative thrust is the theoretical understanding that children are reliable informants of their own experience (Danby and Baker 2001), are capable of engaging in research conversations with adult researchers and, indeed, have the right to do so (see Archard 1993; Franklin 1995; Freeman 1996; Babbie 1998; Kimmel 1988). This chapter deals with a key aspect of the research conversation, that is, the 'opening' of the conversation, where the researcher and potential participant consider the possibility of the conversation and what it might entail for each of them.

The Australian research ethics commentator, Robert Cribb (2004), argues that the research conversation is a discussion partnership, equal in scholarly standing to experimentation and survey, whereby both researcher and participant have the potential to contribute to the generation of data and interpretation. In research ethics parlance, the conversation opening is characteristically an important part of the process of gaining the participant's 'informed consent' to be part of the ensuing conversation. No less important is the possibility of unwillingness to be involved or withdrawal from involvement, situations described by Morrow and Richards (1996: 95) as 'informed dissent' which allow for the participant to refuse to participate or to absent themselves from the research once it is under way. We concur with Weithorn and Scherer (1994: 137) who point out that 'the moral and ethical considerations that apply to adults deciding whether to volunteer ... also pertain to children'. However, as Edwards and Alldred (1999: 267) argue, gaining consent is 'not simply a matter of transferring power from one group (researchers/adults) to another (research subjects/children)... power is not packageable and therefore givable in this sense'. Nor is it a matter of simplifying or downsizing, for children, procedures that are used with adults (Koocher and Keith-Spiegel 1994). Rather, the research conversation and its opening offer the possibility of acknowledging that children have the right to be considered as competent and legitimate participants in the research enterprise.

This perspective is located in an approach to childhood research known as the sociology of childhood. As such, this notion of children's competence in research flies in the face of traditional understandings of children's competence derived from twentieth-century child development and developmental psychology. This perspective highlighted the limitations imposed by children's developmental levels (see Keith-Spiegel 1983; Touliatos and Compton 1983; Hughes and Helling 1991; Koocher and Keith-Spiegel 1994; Hoagwood *et al.* 1996). In other words, by virtue of their developmental level, children were often seen to be short of the requisite capacity to consent to research (Abramovitch *et al.* 1991). The sociology of childhood, on the other hand, provides a different set of understandings of children's competence to engage in research (see Alanen and Mayall 2001; Corsaro 1997; Danby and Baker 1998; James *et al.* 1998; Mayall 2003; Prout and James 1997; Waksler 1991). Here children are seen to be competent in their own right, capable of indicating their willingness or otherwise to engage in the research and capable of contributing to the veracity of the research data. That children have rights to (agree to) participate in research as competent informants of their own experience is a departure from such understandings of research with young children. New perspectives from the sociology of childhood legitimate children's rights to participate in (and withdraw from) research (Danby and Farrell 2004). Such rights reflect, in part, the history of children's rights as human rights. As such, it offers new directions for ethical research with children.

This chapter draws on examples of children's competence as they engage with the authors in opening the research conversation. These conversations are drawn from research that focuses on children's decision-making and experience of governance in their everyday lives. The chapter explicates the reasoning practices found in the communicative strategies of the young participants during the opening turns of the research conversation with an adult interviewer. The analytic resources of talk-in-interaction (Goodwin 2000; Goodwin 1990; Psathas 1995) investigate the social interactions located in the research conversation. Talk is seen as a social interaction and not a one-speaker phenomenon (Psathas 1995). Thus, laughter and even silences are considered important features for analysis (Goodwin 2000; Jacoby and Ochs 1995). This approach examines children's talk in order to investigate their own reasoning methods for making sense of the research situation.

The premise that talk should be examined as a topic in its own right means that the situated performances of the research participants, both child and adult, are under scrutiny. This analytic position provides for the investigation of children's interactions as sites for categorization work. Membership categorization is an effective analytic tool used within studies of talk-in-interaction to investigate how members of particular groups recognize themselves and others as belonging to collections of categories that describe people (Hester and Eglin 1997;, Sacks 1995). Sacks (1995) describes how membership categorization works. In the description 'The baby cried. The mommy picked it up.' (Sacks 1995: 199), Sacks points out that the hearer hears the *mommy* as the mother of the crying baby. This understanding presumes that the categories of *mommy* and *baby* come from a collection of categories called *family*, which can include baby, mommy, and daddy. Category-bound activities refer to the activities that members do (Sacks 1991). Crying, then, is a category-bound activity for a baby. Thus, if an adult cries, they can be called a baby (Silverman 1998). In this way, certain activities are said to be owned by certain members (Sharrock 1974).

In this chapter, we take up this concept of category work to ask how you 'do' being a researcher and how you 'do' being a child participant in a research situation. What are the everyday practices of research participants as they orient to the social and moral order of research? Both researcher and child orient to a number of institutional categories, including being researcher and participant, being child and adult, and being information-giver and information-receiver. By investigating the practices of the children as they display their credentials as research participants, we make visible how both child and researcher orient to the particular social and moral order of the research enterprise.

Membership categorizaton analysis studies the construction of particular moral activities and social relations. For example, Danby and Emmison (2005) investigate 'morality-in-action' when a teenage female caller and the helpline counsellor attribute motives for her actions of forging a medical certificate. The first proposal, that the caller is a normal teenager attempting to fool the teachers, and the second, that evil spirits propelled her against her will, each offer possible moral implications. Moral work in action shows how these categories are produced and organized. The construction of social and moral order occurs within everyday interactions, including the research conversation, and this chapter shows how both the child participant and researcher orient to this moral work.

Our initial interest: 'in heaven'

The research study, conducted under the auspices of the Australian Research Council, investigates the everyday lives of children in Australia and how they experience governance in their homes, schools and communities. Governance, in our work, is defined as the complex and intersecting systems of regulation that operate to show up frames of relevance for children's everyday participation and active engagement in sites such as school, home and community (Danby and Farrell 2002). The research reported in this chapter is drawn from a subset of data consisting of the opening conversations of research interviews with 16 children aged 5–11 years in two primary schools. The children were invited to engage in informal (audio-recorded) conversations about their experiences of decision-making throughout the day and to represent these experiences on a timeline of their day. This chapter reports these conversations that the researchers had with the children about the consent process and about the research enterprise. As such, this chapter does not report directly on the conversations about governance but rather seeks to explicate some of the research practices of gaining children's informed consent in research.

Each participant provided written consent to participate in the study by signing their name or making their special mark, or signature, on the consent form included in the information and consent packages (see Appendix 5B). This was in addition to the parent or guardian providing written consent for their child to participate. In gaining their consent, the information packages were distributed to the children to take home. We then visited the classrooms and spoke directly with the children about the study. The children took this opportunity to ask questions about the study itself and the research activities, and about us as researchers. One boy indicated that, while he wished to participate, his parents did not give permission. This raised theoretical questions about adults contesting or even thwarting children's desire to participate as emblematic of adult governance of children's lives.

One consideration that arose for us in the transcription process was deciding how to identify the speakers (see Appendix 5A for a description of the transcript conventions). Should first names of all participants, children and researcher alike, be used? Should the speakers be labelled Speaker A and Speaker B? Should the terms 'researcher' and 'research participant' be used? The conventions used to represent the participants provides a description that is not neutral but theoretically driven (Baker 1998; Ochs 1979). As Baker (1998: 110) notes, 'transcription assigns a social, political, or moral order to the scene being transcribed'. In the analysis of the opening sequences discussed in this chapter, we refer to the 'researcher' in the third person. In this instance, we applied a 'commonsense meaning' (Baker 1998) that the children and researchers appeared to be using with each other. In other words, we drew predominantly upon the relevant category pair of 'researcher–child's name' to assign a commonsense hearing to these relevant categories. While we have assigned a single membership category, we are aware that both researcher and child participant orient to multiple categories and their associated category-bound activities within the conversations themselves.

In the opening moments of the research conversation, the researcher reviewed the consent form with the child to ensure that they still wanted to participate, and reminded them of their right to drop out of the study at any time without any questions being asked. By inviting the children in this way to reaffirm their decision to participate, consent continued to be constructed as ongoing throughout the research. This research orientation allowed the children themselves to act as gatekeepers of the research (Alderson 2000; Danby 1997). However, affirmation to participate, as we show later in this chapter, is only one of the ways in which children act as gatekeepers of their own experiences.

Many children described this experience of providing consent as a new experience in their lives, as well as a positive experience (Danby *et al.* 2004). Jacob's use of the metaphor of being 'in heaven' describes his pleasure in being asked to provide consent.

Researcher:	how did you feel about actually being asked if you wanted to do it or if you didn't want to do it?
Jacob:	I was in heaven.
Researcher:	Yeah ((laughter)) how come?
Jacob:	Usually I don't get uhmm decisions about those particular things like in school.

It was this response by Jacob that prompted our decision to look more closely at these openings in the audio-recorded research conversations we had collected. As Danby *et al.* (2005), examining openings to conversations shows the ways in which participants initially orient to and display awareness of the particular interactional context under way.

The consent form

The activity of children signing consent forms typically has not been part of the research agenda with young children. Conventionally, once parents have given their permission, children are then invited to engage in the research process without additional discussions about their consent and involvement. As discussed earlier, research into child consent is a relatively new phenomenon and relatively little is known about how the researcher engages with the child in those initial moments of the research interview before the interview proper begins. The children each had the opportunity to provide a consent signature. The responses varied enormously:

- symbol (e.g. flower, star, snowman);
- initials of first and last name;

- cursive handwriting (as opposed to printing name);
- nickname;
- code name (such as an action hero);
- embellished writing (swirls, little pictures);
- first name in full with last name initialled;
- abbreviated name.

At the beginning of each conversation, the researcher began by asking the child participants if they had been informed about the research project. This is a typical research protocol for all participants, including adult participants. Additionally, the researcher explicitly asked about the consent process, showing an orientation to the normative view that children may be unknowing about the research process. In this way, the researcher oriented to the assumed category-bound activity of child participants being possibly unaware of research protocols. In this way, she engaged in the category-bound activity of explaining protocols in specific ways.

Some children, such as Shaun and Fred, explained very clearly their understanding.

Researcher:	and so is that sort of stuff still okay with you
Fred:	yeah
Shaun:	mm
Fred:	so they could write a book about us
Researcher:	mm hm
Fred:	and if we could actually buy the book then we wouldn't even know that it'd be us (0.4)
Researcher:	yep that's pretty much how it works the idea is that we protect your privacy by changing your name to a different name that's called a a pseudonym (0.2) when you don't use the real names
Fred:	yeah

Other children, such as Oralee, used this opening part of the conversation to clarify an aspect of the research study. In the extract below, we observe Oralee engaging the category-bound activity of being a research participant by clarifying the procedures of the research conversation with the researcher.

Researcher:	you do do you remember anything else about the form did you read it
Oralee:	no haha

Researcher:	well the form (0.2) um for you to sign was saying that it was okay by you if you came along and had a conversation with myself or with Ann or with Susan they're the other people that are doing the conversations as well
Oralee:	do we do it with everybody or just one person
Researcher:	no just one person Ann and Sue didn't come today
Oralee:	oh okay

In this way we see that both researcher and child participant are held accountable as they orient to their rights and responsibilities (Freebody 2003) as they 'do' being a researcher and being a research participant. Clarifying is neither primarily a child nor an adult activity, but a research question that could be asked either by child or adult research participant. In this way, the category-bound act of 'clarifying' belongs to the category of 'research participant' and thus blurs the conventional category-bound activities associated with being an adult or being a child.

The activity of consent

In examining the openings to the research conversations, we observe how the child participants reported the activity of signing the consent forms. Within the category of children, a common collection of categories relates to the membership categorization device 'family' and an associated device 'stage-of-life' (Sacks 1995). Within the device 'family', a number of categories are clustered together: family, dad, mum and siblings. When operating within the device 'stage-of-life', children can be described to show development from being a baby to being an adult, along with all the associated activities of key milestones. In the extract below, Sally appears to be orienting to the stage-of-life category when she explains about the signing of her form.

Researcher:	remember it was this form here let's see if we can find yours ((rustling form)) Sally that's your form and did you read this form Sally
Sally:	my ah I didn't read it my dad did
Researcher:	oh okay and did he read any of it to you
Sally:	no
Researcher:	no
Sally:	he just signed it
Researcher:	and I noticed you signed it as well
Sally:	yeah

The father's activity of signing the form can be described as the father engaging in the activities of being a parent. As legal guardian, he gives consent or otherwise. The father, by not asking Sally about her desire to participate, might also be observed as operating within the stage-of-life category where children are understood as being neither responsible nor competent to make decisions about participation in the study. Sally, too, could be described as also operating within this stage-of-life category, as she seems to accept the father's course of action. What is produced here is a child who accepts, seemingly without question, the category-bound activity of having someone make the decision for her to participate. This construction is quite different from that of Tim's, discussed next. Here, Tim constructs himself as one who is a competent research participant, one who reads the consent package and then actively decides to participate.

Researcher:	uh huh (.) ah did you read it
Tim:	um yeah I read it
Researcher:	uh huh (0.8) okay a:and do you remember anything about what you were reading or what you were doing when you signed your name
	(1.0)
Tim:	what I was doing when I was signing it
Researcher:	mm
Tim:	with a friend
	(0.4)
Researcher:	oh you did it with a friend
Tim:	oh (0.2) well yeah
Researcher:	one of the friends from school here
Tim:	yeah
Researcher:	oh okay who was that
Tim:	um Terry he didn't
Researcher:	okay
Tim:	do
Researcher:	oh okay so did Terry make the decision not to participate
Tim:	yeah I think so
Researcher:	a:and
Tim:	( )
Researcher:	did you make the decision that you were going to participate
	(0.8)
Researcher:	okay well I might just remind you what the form is about because the idea is that when you (0.2) sign your name here or put your special (.) mark your signature

	the idea is that that's your way of showing (0.4) us the people doing the study
Tim:	mm
Researcher:	that you're okay about participating in the study
Tim:	yeah

Here, Tim has produced an account where he is a research participant who knows what the study is about, and about the responsibilities of being a research participant. Further, his account does not refer to any parent involvement, although this would have been necessary, as the consent form required signed parental approval. Tim's account is heard to invoke the characteristics and responsibilities of an informed research participant and not the stage-of-life category of child being dependent upon adults for authorization. The pairing of the categories of researcher and research participant makes absent the pairing of other categories, such as child–parent or teacher–student. In other words, we see a different social order being constructed between researcher and child from that which had been established between researcher and Sally.

The pedagogic work of the researcher

In the opening turns of the conversations, the researcher asks a number of questions about how the children felt when they signed the forms. She also asks the children if they have had to sign other permission forms. This might be an unusual set of questions when an adult researcher interviews an adult participant. However, the researcher appears to be orienting to the children's experiences (or lack thereof), as consent signatures typically are not part of a young child's repertoire of experience. The researcher also uses these questions as a pedagogic activity to teach about consent and permission forms more generally. Her questioning produces accounts from the children about their range of experiences, in which they indicated that, routinely, they had little or no opportunities to engage in signing consent or permission forms. This is very clearly shown by Arnold in the extract below:

	okay and um so what did you think about this form that ah only actually asked for the student's signature it didn't actually have a space for a parent signature it what did you think of that
Researcher:	
Arnold:	o:oh I was quite surprised
Researcher:	oh yeah

The researcher, while suggesting that it is unusual for children to sign their own forms, also helps to normalize this experience. She relates the occurrence of signing the research consent form with the signing of other forms.

Researcher: to participate (0.4) is that a new experience for you
               or have you received a form like this another time
Shaun: ummm not really (0.4) I haven't really had one
               (1.0)
Researcher: have you (0.2) ever had experience with any other
               sorts of forms where somebody has to sign
Shaun: um (.) a couple of times actually for soccer and stuff
Researcher: okay and with soccer did you have to sign
Shaun: no I didn't but yeah
Researcher: did anyone have to sign the soccer [form
Shaun: [I think my mum did and my dad
Researcher: [oh okay because that seems to be a little more
               common that children get forms that they then
               take to their parents and their parents [and]
Shaun: [yeah

In this way, the researcher refers to a norm as a way of explain an activity 'that seems to be a little more common', that of signing other types of consent forms (the soccer form). In this way, the specific use of this norm provides a sense of proper orderliness to this activity (Hester 2000; Sacks 1992, 1995; Silverman 1998). This also invokes the relevant membership categorization to identify the 'doer' of the activity (Hester 2000; Sacks 1995). The 'doer' is thus engaging properly in the activity of signing forms, whether that is the permission form for soccer or the consent form for research. Thus, signing the consent form becomes an accountable and orderly matter.

There is certainly evidence to show that children play an active role in the research agenda and themselves act as gatekeepers (Danby 1997; Cobb *et al.* 2005), but this has not been necessarily an explicit and valued recognition. In the next extract, the researcher's question positions Lilly in terms of how she felt about signing the consent form. Lilly's first response was to indicate that she 'didn't know' how she felt about signing the forms. This initial reply is designed by Lilly in such a way as to shut down any information-giving; in other words, Lilly acts as gatekeeper to her own experiences and reasoning practices. However, the researcher does not accept this, and asks further 'were you interested'. The researcher's question here is one designed to elicit a preferred response (Sacks 1987) from Lilly. That is, this type of questioning by the researcher can create preferred answers (Silverman 1998). After a short pause, Lilly agrees that she was:

Researcher:	Lilly do you remember signing the consent form that came from university
Lilly:	yep
Researcher:	mmhm and how did you feel about that about being asked if you wanted to join in the activities
Lilly:	I don't know
Researcher:	were you interested
	(0.4)
Lilly:	yeah
Researcher:	mmhm
Researcher:	and um there was a space on the form for you to sign your name
Lilly:	mmhm
Researcher:	do you normally sign your name on forms
Lilly:	no (1.0) not really

Central to this interaction is the assumption by the researcher that Lilly can be an expert witness to her own feelings and reasoning practices, that is, she orients to Lilly as 'research participant in action'. As the research conversation continues with Lilly, we see a 'category transformation' (Hester 2000: 216). The category of an unknowing child who was unaware of how she felt about being asked to participate is now transformed into a category that recognizes the importance of being an active decision-maker and participant. This is achieved by her reporting that she felt '(it means) sort of like I'm important. It's for me. I have to sign':

Lilly:	Uhmmm well you don't normally get to sign your name on contracts normally (it's just) ohhh your parents have to sign or a teacher has to sign, and somebody else has to sign or something like that.
Researcher:	Uh-huh. And how did you feel when you got to sign?
Lilly:	(it means) sort of like I'm important. It's for me. I have to sign.
Researcher:	Ahhh okay. So you thought it was a good thing to have to do?
Lilly:	Yeah
Researcher:	And what did your parents think about you signing?
Lilly:	Cause then they know that I wanna do it not just them
Researcher:	That's right

Lilly:	Because if you just have your parents signing it sorta seems like some children don't even wanna do it they just want (.) their parents just want (.) to do to do it so, this way you have to get y- y children to actually do it to make sure that you want to do it.
Researcher:	Mhmm mhmm. And why did you want to do the study?
Lilly:	Uhmmm I don't know, I just like to try things.

Lilly's comment that the activity of signing the consent form made her feel important is an account that was also noted by others. For example, Shaun also described how he felt when he was asked.

Researcher:	what do you think of that
	(2.4)
Shaun:	yeah I like it
Researcher:	uh huh [allright
Shaun:	[it gives you a bit more responsibility
Researcher:	beg your pardon
Shaun:	it's like giving the person (0.2) a bit more responsibility
Researcher:	[okay and do you feel like it gave you a bit more responsibility
Shaun:	[(--) yeah (.) sort of

What is evident in these extracts is that the researcher's orientation to the children as research participants elicited the pairing of the categories of being a researcher and being a research participant. Being a child research participant, then, elicits the category-bound activities of feeling important and being responsible.

Conclusion

Our examination of these opening conversations in the research interview has shown how both the researcher and child collaboratively produce an account of the consent process. This investigation has made visible the moral work involved in the ethical process of gaining consent from research participants who are also children. To date, this has been an area of research and ethics that has been largely invisible. By investigating how the researcher and child participants conducted the research conversations, and how they engaged with each other, we show how they organized the talk-in-action collaboratively to make sense of the research conversation. In order to do this, certain attributes are brought to light by both researcher and participant.

First, children are gatekeepers of their own accounts. Children were competent to withhold or share their experiences, were able to clarify aspects of the study, and ultimately decided whether or not they chose to participate. For example, Lilly showed very clearly that she was the gate-keeper of her own experiences, even though her parents had provided formal consent. At first Lilly withheld her account, saying that she 'didn't know' how she felt, but later explained to the researcher that signing the consent form had made her feel 'important'. The close investigation of these first turns shows how critical the first moments of the researcher conversation are in establishing the social order of the research interview.

Second, the researcher worked from at least two moral perspectives. She avoided making any explicit moral evaluations about the participatory decision-making activities of the child or parent. However, within her talk was an explicit moral orientation that the children were competent to report their own experiences. This indicates the theoretical stance of the researcher, where she viewed the children as competent witnesses to their own experiences. In this way, the children's accounts were purposefully designed for the recipient, the researcher. In other words, the children attended to the researcher-designed category of 'research participant in action'. In offering the children a social interactional space to be competent research participants, the researcher established a different type of social order from one where children are assumed to be unknowing participants. In offering this type of interaction, we can see how the social order of the research enterprise is constructed. At first, the activity of consent signing seemed quite an unusual experience, but the researcher oriented to this by normalizing this activity to other aspects of daily life, such as signing up for soccer.

Third, both researcher and child participant collaboratively produced the interview. These conversation openings illustrate not only the ethical protocol of consent but also how the researcher and child participant accomplished the moral work of ' "who" they relevantly "are" ' (Freebody 2003: 162) from a range of possible categorizations. Both children and researcher oriented to a number of categories. In this way, the research focus was more than a content analysis of what was said, but also an investigation of how researcher and child together produced their accounts. In this way, we saw a blurring of the typical child–adult interactions, as children were able to clarify aspects of the research study, as might any research participant, whether they were child or adult.

This chapter has identified key considerations for research with young children. The ethical and moral considerations that apply to adults when they decide to be research participants also apply to children. The processes of children participating in the research enterprise involve researchers listening to children regarding events and experiences that relate to them. This demands respecting children from their own standpoints (Butler 1996; Mayall 2002). Such a perspective involves describing children's everyday experiences in ways that recognize them as competent witnesses to their own lives. It is this perspective that drives our research on governance of the lives of children, allowing us to generate, with them, their own accounts of their everyday experience. This tenet of our work is central to sociological understandings of childhood. As such, it has the potential to offer new directions for ethical research with children.

References

Abramovitch, R., Freedman, J., Thoden, K. and Nikolich, C. (1991) Children's capacity to consent to participation in psychological research: Empirical findings, *Child Development*, 62: 1100–9.

Alanen, L. and Mayall, B. (eds.) (2001) *Conceptualizing Child–Adult Relations.*, London: RoutledgeFalmer.

Alderson, P. (2000) Children as researchers: the effects of participation rights on research methodology, in P. Christensen and A. James (eds) *Research with Children: Perspectives and Practices*. London: Falmer Press.

Archard, D. (1993) *Children, Rights and Childhood*. London: Routledge.

Australian Human Rights Commission/Australian Law Reform Commission (1997) *Seen and Heard Report. Children in Australia's Legal Processes*. Canberra: AHRC/ALRC.

Babbie, E. (1998) *The Practice of Social Research*. Belmont, CA: Wadsworth.

Baker, C. (1998) Transcription and representation in literacy research, in J. Flood, S.B. Heath and D. Lapp (eds) *A Handbook for Literacy Educators: Research on Teaching the Communicative and Visual Arts* (pp. 108–18). New York: Macmillan.

Butler, I. (1996) Children and the sociology of childhood, in I. Butler and I. Shaw (eds) *A Case of Neglect? Children's Experiences and the Sociology of Childhood*. Avebury: Aldershot.

Clark, A., McQuail, S. and Moss, P. (2003) *Exploring the Field of Listening to and Consulting with Young Children*. London: DfES.

Cobb, C., Danby, S. and Farrell, A. (2005). Governance of children's everyday spaces, *Australian Journal of Early Childhood*, 30(1): 14–20.

Corsaro, W.A. (1997) *The Sociology of Childhood*. Thousand Oaks, CA: Pine Forge Press.

Cribb, R. (2004) Ethical regulation and humanities research in Australia: Problems and consequences, *Monash Bioethics Review*, 23(3): 39–57.

Danby, S. (1997) The observer observed, the researcher researched: the reflexive nature of phenomena, in *Proceedings of the Australian Association for Research in Education Conference*, Brisbane, November–December.

Danby, S. and Baker, C. (1998) 'What's the problem?' Restoring social order in the preschool classroom, in I. Hutchby and J. Moran-Ellis (eds) *Children and Social Competence: Arenas of Action* (pp. 157–86). London: Falmer Press.

Danby, S. and Baker, C. (2001) Escalating terror: communicative strategies in a preschool classroom dispute, *Early Education and Development*, 12(3): 343–58.

Danby, S. and Emmison, M. (2005) Kids, counsellors and troubles-telling: Morality-in-action in talk on an Australian children's helpline, in J.C.M. Tholander (eds) *Children, Morality and Interaction*. Hauppauge, NY: Nova Science (in press).

Danby, S. and Farrell, M.A. (2002) Children's accounts of adult-determined regulation on their everyday experiences. Paper presented to the Australian Association for Education Research Conference, Brisbane, 1–5 December.

Danby, S. and Farrell, A. (2004) Accounting for young children's competence in educational research: New perspectives on research ethics, *Australian Educational Researcher*, 31(3): 35–49.

Danby, S., Farrell, A., Powell, K. and Leiminer, M. (2004) *Children's Accounts of Governance in Their Everyday Lives*. Technical paper to schools in ATN Research. Brisbane: QUT.

Danby, S., Baker, C.D. and Emmison, M. (2005) Four observations on openings in calls to Kids Help Line, in C. Baker, A. Firth and M. Emmison (eds) *Calling for Help*. Amsterdam: John Benjamins (in press).

Edwards, R. and Alldred, P. (1999) Children and young people's views of social research. The case of research on home–school relations, *Childhood*, 6(2): 261–81.

Franklin, B. (1995) *Handbook of Children's Rights: Comparative Policy and Practice*. London: Routledge.

Freebody, P. (2003) *Qualitative Research in Education: Interaction and Practice*. London: Sage.

Freeman, M. (ed.) (1996) *Children's Rights: A Comparative Perspective*, Brookfield, VT: Dartmouth.

Goodwin, C. (2000) Action and embodiment within situated human interaction, *Journal of Pragmatics*, 32: 1489-1522.

Goodwin, M.H. (1990) *He-Said-She-Said: Talk as Social Organization among Black Children*. Bloomington: Indiana University Press.

Hester, S. (2000) The local order of deviance in school: Membership categorization, motives and morality in referral talk, in S. Hester and D. Francis (eds) *Local Educational Order* (pp. 197–222). Amsterdam: John Benjamins.

Hester, S. and Eglin, P. (1997) Membership categorization: An introduction, in S. Hester and P. Eglin (eds) *Culture in Action: Studies of Membership Categorization* (pp. 1–23). Washington, DC: International Institute for Ethnomethodology and Conversation Analysis and University Press of America.

Hoagwood, K., Jensen, P. and Fisher, C. (eds) (1996) *Ethical Issues in Mental Health Research with Children and Adolescents*. Mahwah, NJ: Lawrence Erlbaum Associates.

Hughes, T. and Helling, M. (1991) A case for obtaining informed consent from young children, *Early Childhood Research Quarterly*, 6: 225–32.

Jacoby, S. and Ochs, E. (1995) Co-construction: An introduction, *Research on Language and Social Interaction*, 28(3): 171–83.

James, A., Jenks, C. and Prout, A. (1998) *Theorising Childhood*. Cambridge: Polity Press.

Keith-Spiegel, P. (1983) Children and consent to participate in research, in G.B. Melton, G.P. Koocher and M.J. Saks (eds) *Children's Competence to Consent* (pp. 179–211). New York: Plenum.

Kimmel, A.J. (1988) *Ethics and Values in Applied Social Research*. Newbury Park, CA: Sage Publications.

Koocher, G.P. and Keith-Spiegel, P. (1994) Scientific issues in psychosocial and educational research with children, in M.A. Grodin and L.H. Glantz (eds) *Children as Research Subjects: Science, Ethics and Law* (pp. 47–80). New York: Oxford University Press.

MacNaughton, G., Smith, K. and Lawrence, H. (2004) *Hearing Young Children's Voices. ACT Children's Strategy. Consultation with Children Birth to Eight Years of Age*. Canberra: Department of Education, Youth and Family Services.

Malone, S. (2003) Ethics at home: Informed consent in your own backyard. *Qualitative Studies in Education*, 16(6): 797–815.

Mayall, B. (2002) *Towards Sociology for Childhood: Thinking from Children's Lives*. Buckingham: Open University Press.

Mayall, B. (2003) *Sociologies of Childhood and Educational Thinking*. London: Institute of Education University of London.

Morrow, V. and Richards, M. (1996) The ethics of social research with children: An overview, *Children & Society*, 10: 90–105.

Ochs, E. (1979) Transcription as theory, in E. Ochs and B.B. Schieffelin (eds) *Developmental Pragmatics* (pp. 43–72). New York: Academic Press.

Prout, A. and James, A. (1997) A new paradigm for the sociology of childhood? Provenance, promise and problems, in A. James and A. Prout (eds) *Constructing and Reconstructing Childhood: Contemporary Issues in the Sociological Study of Childhood*, 2nd edn (pp. 7–33). London: Falmer Press.

Psathas, G. (1995) *Conversation Analysis: The Study of Talk-in-Interaction*. Thousand Oaks, CA: Sage.

Sacks, H. (1987) On the preferences for agreement and contiguity in sequences in conversation, in G. Button and J.R.E. Lee (eds) *Talk and Social Organization* (pp. 54–69). Clevedon: Multilingual Matters.

Sacks, H. (1991) On the analysability of stories by children, in F.C. Waksler (ed.) *Studying the Social Worlds of Children: Sociological Readings* (pp. 195–215). London: Falmer Press.

Sacks, H. (1992) *Lectures on Conversation* (ed. G. Jefferson). Oxford: Blackwell.

Sacks, H. (1995) *Lectures on Conversation, Volumes I and II* (ed. G. Jefferson). Oxford: Blackwell.

Sharrock, W.W. (1974) On owning knowledge, in R. Turner (ed.) *Ethnomethodology: Selected Readings* (pp. 45–53). Harmondsworth: Penguin.

Silverman, D. (1998) *Harvey Sacks: Social Science and Conversation Analysis.* Cambridge: Polity Press.

Stafford, A., Laybourn, A., Hill, M. and Walker, M. (2003) 'Having a say': Children and young people talk about consultation, *Children & Society*, 17: 361–73.

Tayler, C., Farrell, A., Tennent, L. and Patterson, C. (2004) Child and family hubs and social capital, *Commission for Children and Young People Issues Paper*, 3: 1–7.

Touliatos, J. and Compton, N.H. (1983) *Approaches to Child Study.* Minneapolis, MN: Burgess.

Waksler, F. (1991) Studying children: phenomenological insights, in F. Waksler (ed.) *Studying the Social Worlds of Children: Sociological Readings* (pp. 60–9). London: Falmer Press.

Weithorn, L.A. and Scherer, D.G. (1994) Children's involvement in research participation decisions: Psychological considerations, in M.A. Grodin and L. Glanz (eds) *Children as Research Subjects: Science, Ethics and Law* (pp. 133–79). New York: Oxford University Press.

Appendix 5A Transcript Notation

Data are transcribed using a system created by Jefferson and described in Psathas (1995). The following are the features used in these transcripts:

( )	word(s) spoken but not audible
(was)	best guess for word(s) spoken
(( ))	transcriber's description
voice	normal speaking voice
voice	increased volume
[	two speakers' turns overlap at this point
=	no interval between turns
do:on't	sound extended
(2.0)	pause timed in seconds

Appendix 5B Consent Form

CONSENT FORM

RESEARCH PROJECT: CHILDREN'S ACCOUNTS OF GOVERNANCE IN
EVERYDAY LIVES

I am willing to talk with Ann, Susan or Kathy and other kids about how
much I get to decide what I do in my everyday life. I am also willing to do
a timeline of the activities I do in a day.

It is OK by me that:
1   our conversations and the timeline activity will not name or identify
    me;
2   our conversations and the timeline activity will be tape recorded;
3   only Ann, Susan and Kathy will use the tapes and will keep them in
    a locked filing cabinet at (   ) for 5 years and then destroy them;
4   I can drop out of the study at any time without any questions being
    asked;
5   Ann, Susan or Kathy might talk to someone responsible if they are
    worried about my safety.

My name

My signature or special mark   ....✳..................

Today's date   ....*24 / 10 / 02*..........

6   Researching sensitive issues
Kerryann Walsh

This chapter uses accounts of research into child abuse and neglect to illustrate some of the ethical issues involved in sensitive research. It refers to three major studies of teachers' work in child abuse and neglect (Walsh 1995, 2002; Walsh *et al.* 2004). Key ethical issues encountered in these studies include:

- individual resistance to research;
- institutional obstruction of research;
- identifying children who are experiencing or may be at risk of abuse and neglect;
- engaging participants in research;
- dealing with research gatekeepers.

Some research with children can be sensitive in the sense that it is capable of arousing strong feelings and reactions. But more than this, sensitive research can involve a measure of risk to participants which 'renders problematic the collection, holding and/or dissemination of research data' (Lee and Renzetti 1993: 4). Further, the sensitivities of such research can produce methodological complexities, ethical dilemmas and safety concerns (see Brewer 1993). While these are not limited to research on sensitive topics, they are more acute when sensitivities exist.

Traditionally, research methods texts rarely expose ethical and practical problems in sensitive research. However, in the last decade work from social and health research (Hood *et al.* 1999; Miller *et al.* 2003) and early childhood education (Hatch 1995; Aubrey *et al.* 2000) has exposed the difficulties of conducting sensitive child-related research. Researchers contemplating sensitive research must recognize that issues may arise at any stage of the research process, from gaining ethical clearance, to data collection, writing up and disseminating results. Throughout the research process, researchers must safeguard the rights of participants in the research, consider the representations of individuals and groups in the data, and anticipate potential consequences of the research even more thoroughly than in other types of research (David 1993; Herzberger 1993).

Research into child abuse and neglect is inherently sensitive (see Herzberger 1993). There is sensitivity in:

- research with children who are known to have experienced abuse or neglect;
- research with children who may be at risk of abuse or neglect;
- research with teachers who have known about or suspected child abuse and neglect; and
- research with teachers about their knowledge of child abuse and neglect, and their teaching practices relating to prevention of and intervention in child abuse and neglect.

The first two categories of research with children have been discussed extensively (Gibbons *et al.* 1995). This chapter focuses on research with children's teachers, a focus which has received less attention.

The sensitivity of research with children's teachers about child abuse and neglect is evident in at least four ways (see Lee and Renzetti 1993). First, it enters areas that are private and personal. Research has consistently shown that teachers can be reluctant to report child abuse and neglect because they respect family privacy and they worry about the quality of any consequent intervention into families' lives (Abrahams *et al.* 1992; Campbell and Wigglesworth 1993; Tite 1993; O'Toole *et al.* 1999; Hinson and Fossey 2000). Second, it deals with harmful behaviours and practices which, if exposed, could adversely affect teachers' reputations and incriminate parents or other school/centre staff. Studying how teachers handle child abuse and neglect risks them revealing their own and others' appropriate and inappropriate practices (Kenny 2001), and the lawful and unlawful activities of themselves, their colleagues, and parents of children in their care. Third, it challenges established ways of dealing with problems and the vested interests of institutions. Research into teachers' work and knowledge in child abuse and neglect has questioned the adequacy of policy, professional development and support services (Walsh 2002). Fourth, it deals with values and ideals that are important to participants. Research has confronted teachers' own ideas about appropriate discipline of children (Tite 1993, 1994) and their long-held, value-laden notions of childhood and families (Kitzinger 1990; Walkerdine 1999; Johnson 2000).

Additionally, the literature confirms that child abuse and neglect arouses strong emotions such as shock, denial, sympathy, pity, frustration, anger, blame, distress and anxiety, guilt and self-recrimination, sadness and depression, revulsion, horror, disgust, revenge and the desire for punishment (Briggs and Hawkins 1997). These may fuel resistance and obstruction to sensitive research.

Individual resistance to sensitive research

Research involving children's teachers should observe general ethical principles such as obtaining consent, doing no harm, minimizing potentially stressful situations for participants, and respecting the beliefs, attitudes, wishes and rights of the participants, including the right to refuse participation or to withdraw from the project at any time (Bibby 1997; Miller and Crabtree 1999; Aubrey *et al.* 2000). These are important ethical issues that should underpin research of any kind. However, even when these principles are observed, individuals can resist participating in research.

Recruiting participants for the Logan Teacher Study (Walsh 2002) was a case in point. This study formed the first two of three phases in my doctoral research. The main research question was 'How do early childhood teachers work with children with a history of abuse and neglect; and what knowledge do they use to guide them in this work?'. I first obtained university ethics clearance (from the University Human Research Ethics Committee) and institutional approvals to conduct the research. Then I invited several hundred early childhood teachers to participate in the study by mailing information to some 200 early childhood care and education workplaces in a geographical area known to have a high incidence of child abuse and neglect. The information asked teachers for responses indicating willingness to participate. No teachers responded.

To understand this zero response rate, later described as a *silence*, I interviewed a small number of staff from care and education settings and child protection agencies in the area. I recruited these participants through my own professional networks. In this second phase I wanted to investigate the reasons for teachers' resistance to the first approach. Six themes emerged from these interviews, and these themes were used to generate a follow-up survey of the originally targeted services.

The second phase survey generated a 40 per cent response rate (for response rates in such research, see Crenshaw *et al.* 1995; Tite 1994; Shor 1997; Van Haeringen *et al.* 1998). I identified six reasons for teachers' unwillingness or inability to participate. In descending order of frequency these were: they did not receive the initial invitation; they did not have time to participate in the research; they thought they did not fit the criteria for participation because they believed they did not have abused or neglected children in their classrooms; they did not wish to have their work examined because they were unsure how to handle child abuse and neglect; and they were concerned about confidentiality. A very small proportion of teachers nominated other personal reasons for not participating; one of these related to a teacher's own childhood experience of abuse.

From this, I learned at least three lessons about individual resistance. First, those who open the mail can prevent it reaching targeted participants.

Second, resistance did not imply that teachers were not concerned about the issue. Rather, teachers experience multiple demands on their time. Lack of time is a recurring theme in analyses of teachers' resistance to aspects of their role in child protection. Research has identified lack of time as a factor in the limited implementation of a child abuse prevention curriculum in schools (Hewson *et al.* 1995); in teachers' non-attendance at a child protection training course (Campbell and Macdonald 1996); in teachers lacking opportunities for children to make disclosures of abuse (Smyth 1996); and in limited coverage of child abuse and neglect in teacher education programmes across Australia (Watts and Laskey 1993). Not surprisingly, in our 2004 Queensland survey of teachers' thresholds for identifying and reporting child abuse and neglect, similar reasons explained schools' resistance to participation in the study (Walsh *et al.* 2004). Yet these reasons cannot fully account for teachers' choices to not participate. After all, teachers still choose how to use their time, even when it is limited. To help teachers with their choices, researchers should respect teachers' time. Strategies include piloting survey instruments and interview formats, and accurately briefing potential participants about the amount and type of time involved in participation. Once participants understand the time commitment, researchers must then be prepared for them to exercise their right to participate or not.

Third, teachers may be wary about inquiries into their teaching practice, especially when they perceive deficits in their own knowledge and preparation, and when they lack confidence in dealing with the issue. Almost three decades of research on teachers and child abuse and neglect have documented teachers' unease about the adequacy of their pre-service and in-service training (Volpe 1981; Wurtele and Schmidt 1992; Smyth 1996; Kenny 2001), their difficulties in accurately recognizing the signs and symptoms (Levin 1983; Randolph and Gold 1994; Crenshaw *et al.* 1995) and their confusion about the protocols for making reports (Abrahams *et al.* 1992; Reiniger *et al.* 1995).

Studies of teachers and their practices risk revealing what teachers know and do, and what they do not know and do not do. Researchers should be aware that this can make teachers unreceptive to research, even when confidentiality and anonymity are assured. This does not mean that researchers should be resigned to defeat. On the contrary, there can be a moral imperative that drives us to make sense of these complexities, if we believe that in doing so, we might redress injustice. Despite the best intentions of researchers, however, institutions can reinforce resistance by obstructing research. This too requires examination.

Institutional obstruction to sensitive research

Institutional obstruction to sensitive research can make research so difficult that researchers may consider abandoning it. Obstruction can be subtle, such as stalling the approval process; or it can be overt, such as blatant refusal to participate. In the Logan Teacher Study, I experienced deterrence and stalling. Before obtaining institutional approvals to conduct the research, I had to negotiate with a regional authority to gain access to participants. I was discouraged from proceeding because of concerns that the study could harm the image of early years services in the area by revealing inappropriate practices and drawing attention to the prevalence of child abuse and neglect in the area. Stalling was evident when applications for institutional approvals took up to 9 months to achieve a response.

I learned at least three lessons about institutional obstruction in this process. First, there may be times when it is necessary to describe the nature of the research broadly and express aims and outcomes of research in general terms, so that authorities and potential participants are not unduly dissuaded from participating. This does not mean engaging in deception. Rather, it is about deciding on the purpose and nature of the investigation and nesting it within a broader project. Aubrey *et al.* (2000) suggest this may be appropriate with certain sensitive issues because fully explaining the focus to institutions may limit the research, and opportunities to change a situation may be lost.

Second, institutional obstruction can be theorized. I have experienced institutional obstruction which can silence both researchers and participants. Silence is a frequently used metaphor in the child abuse literature, usually relating to perspectives that adult survivors hold of their treatment as children, rather than perspectives of professionals who work with children. This silence has power. As Nelson (1998: 145) points out, 'the enforcement of silence has been and remains the most potent weapon of abusers, both individually and collectively'.

Third, institutional obstruction is not static. Although restrictive attitudes at one time can prevent professions from learning more about sensitive issues and can constrain researchers from gaining more informed understandings of the issues, this is changeable. In the seven years since the Logan Teacher Study, obstruction of research on child abuse and neglect has been made more difficult with a new socio-political climate, characterized by accountability in the way statutory bodies deal with child abuse and neglect. Inquiries into institutional mishandling of child abuse and neglect (Forde 1999; Criminal Justice Commission 2000; Crime and Misconduct Commission 2004) and high-profile cases of misconduct against schools and school staff (O'Callaghan and Briggs 2003) have forced greater acceptance of external scrutiny of practices, heightened internal monitoring of practice, and led to whole-of-government strategies for promoting safer school environments (Australian Government Department of Education Science and Training 2003).

Identifying child abuse and neglect

In many jurisdictions, those who plan to conduct research with children must obtain a criminal history check before beginning the research to ensure they are suitable for this work (e.g. Queensland's Commission for Children and Young People Act 2000). While most researchers do not set out to uncover new cases of child abuse and neglect, children who are experiencing abuse and neglect, or who may be at risk of it, may be identified during research with their teachers. Researchers must, therefore, be aware of their legal responsibilities to report.

In many parts of the world, legislation specifies those who are compelled to report child abuse and neglect. In these jurisdictions, a person who, in the course of their professional work, knows or suspects (on reasonable grounds) that a child is at risk of harm must report this to designated authorities. Where mandatory reporting obligations exist, responsibility rests with the individual to make a judgement and act upon it. Mandatory reporting legislation in most jurisdictions protects reporters from liability for defamation if reports are made in good faith and later prove to be unsubstantiated (Briggs and Hawkins 1997; New South Wales Commission for Children and Young People 2003). And reports may not be considered a breach of professional ethics.

In rare cases, researchers may find that their discoveries force them to decide how to intervene in unlawful situations, or to decide if they maintain the confidentiality of the participant or report information with potential to cause harm to the safety of individuals. An example of this would be if school or centre staff reveal misconduct by other members of staff. General ethical guidelines for conducting research include obtaining informed consent from participants, but in research with teachers around child abuse and neglect it may be necessary to include a statement indicating that, although confidentiality is assured, legal requirements may mean the researcher having to report certain type of information to relevant authorities.

Sikes (2004: 32) advises that researchers must 'think through eventualities and possibilities and feel confident that insofar as they are able, they have taken all possible precautions to avoid harming and doing wrong to anyone touched by their research'. If encountering previously unidentified child abuse or neglect, the decision about what to do is critical. It is more likely to occur in interview situations than in anonymous surveys. Researchers may find that they receive disclosures about past abuse, and so need to be equipped with resources and referral information appropriate for adult survivors, their friends or relatives. Researchers may also receive disclosures about present abuse: a teacher may discuss a case they are either concerned about or ambivalent about reporting. When this happened in my research, I was able to ask the teacher if they wanted the tape turned off while we discussed this situation in more depth. In other instances I said I would return to a particular comment after the interview and I made a note to do so when the tape was turned off.

Finally, anyone conducting research with children's teachers about child abuse and neglect should be informed about the prevalence and nature of child abuse and neglect and the indicators of various types of maltreatment so that they can report reasonable suspicions in good faith to authorities. When researchers are aware of circumstances in schools or centres that compromise children's safety, they have a duty to inform others who can work to improve the situation. In disseminating the findings from research, researchers should consider situations that may require advocacy or active endeavours to promote intervention and prevention, and make clear recommendations for future action.

Engaging participants in sensitive research

Engaging participants in sensitive research raises methodological questions such as sampling, ethical questions such as participants' rights to privacy, and political questions about individual and institutional preferences for certain types of research. I learned that simply calling for participants does not necessarily yield sufficient interest for the research to proceed.

In my honours research (Walsh 1995) on the issues influencing teachers' reporting of child abuse and neglect, I used a purposive (non-probability) sampling approach, *snowball sampling* (Lincoln and Guba 1985). In this study, I selected a sample from which I could learn the most. I collated the sample by beginning with a small group of early childhood teachers from a network group, who then nominated other teachers considered likely to have reported a case of child abuse or neglect (the criterion for participation in the study). The resulting sample was a relatively homogeneous group of 48 teachers who were interviewed by telephone. Of these, 19 teachers had reported. Of the reporters, 11 volunteered to participate in a longer survey about their decision-making, and of these, eight participated in further semi-structured interviews.

As noted previously, in the second phase of my doctoral study (Walsh 2002) I wanted to find the reasons for teachers' resistance to the first phase of the study. The sample was built from professional networks. The participants represented a non-homogeneous sample by virtue of their employment in care and education settings or child protection agencies. This is *maximum variation sampling* (Patton 1990) which can provide confirming and disconfirming evidence to strengthen the research process and test its findings. Then, in the third phase of my doctoral study (Walsh 2002), I sought a small purposive sample with specific qualities for in-depth interviews about their work with abused and neglected children and the knowledge that guided them in this work. The criteria for selection were critical: experience of supporting and managing abused and neglected children in the classroom; teaching expertise as identified by peers; and motivation and ability to reflect on situations. I looked for individuals who could provide vivid and/or enlightening data: a sampling approach termed *critical case sampling* (Patton 1990).

In the 2004 Child Abuse and Neglect Teacher Questionnaire (Walsh *et al*. 2004), we could not use random sampling methods because we anticipated a high rate of refusal to participate. Yet, we wanted to access as many teachers as possible. We used a type of whole-school *convenience sample*. We began with a population of all government primary schools (*n* = 302) in 13 administrative districts in South East Queensland. We mailed a one-page information sheet about the study to the school administrator in every school. We received approximately 250 surveys and eight teachers volunteered to participate in follow-up interviews. This approach was both cost- and time-effective, and the strategies we used to enlist and maintain schools' cooperation were vital to the success of the project.

Dealing with gatekeepers

Research gatekeepers are those who may give permission for research to proceed, sometimes with specifications that the research be conducted in a particular way (Homan 2002). They provide access to research sites, documents, information and personnel. While their actions may frustrate researchers, gatekeepers – whether ethics committees, school or centre administrators, local authorities, governing boards or management committees – judge the benefits and costs of participating in research, not only for themselves, but also for the teachers, parents and children to whom they are accountable.

In the Logan Teacher Study (Walsh 2002) gatekeepers were staff who opened the mail. They decided what deserved attention and what could be discarded. Some organizations may have gatekeeping policies disallowing participation in certain research, and researchers are not informed about these policies. Obtaining access can be related to issues beyond the project itself and negotiating access may be more difficult at one time than another. For example, sensitivity about a topic is heightened because of media attention. No matter what the researcher's intention, gatekeepers can perceive in some research the possibility of undesirable public attention.

Gatekeepers voiced reservations about this type of research in three main areas:

- concerns about parent perceptions (that parents may easily misinterpret the purpose of the research, or that participation in child abuse research will damage parent–teacher relationships, especially for children at risk);
- fears about damage to school or centre image and loss of market share (because of the negative connotations associated with involvement in child abuse research, or because the community may interpret an undesirably high incidence of child abuse and neglect at a school or centre participating in child abuse research); and
- panic about teacher practices (that research may uncover gaps in teacher knowledge, and/or inappropriate teacher practices such as misconduct).

Real or perceived vulnerabilities, fears and risks have implications for developing openness and trust with gatekeepers. To address the issue of trust, researchers might consider planning how to best maintain anonymity of the school/centre and staff. Researchers should also develop processes for dealing with compromising information, and ways for communicating feedback to research participants. An established way for giving feedback to participants is *member checking*: providing a summary of research findings to participants and allowing them the opportunity to review data and correct errors before researchers make conclusions and disseminate the research (Aubrey *et al*. 2000; Pring 2000). Another process involves providing participants with an executive summary of the final research report. Researchers soon become aware of the power imbalances that are evident in their interactions with gatekeepers. When this power rests in favour of the researcher, it is important that it is used ethically. This is particularly important when the safety and well-being of children are involved and when research findings hold the potential to influence their lives.

Summary

In this chapter I have discussed the sensitivities of research with children's teachers about child abuse and neglect. While researchers may follow general ethical research guidelines, those engaging in sensitive child-related research must do so even more thoroughly than in other types of research. As much as we may wish it to be, research is not always an orderly process. Some hold that the dilemmas encountered in child abuse research can be best resolved by withdrawing from or not conducting such research at all.

However, preventing child abuse and neglect and working towards social justice for children demands research-generated knowledge derived from such work.

Questions for reflection

1   Can any research be sensitive or become sensitive? Under what conditions? Consider your own research. Under what conditions could it become sensitive and why?
2   What is at stake for individuals and institutions in participating in research about their professional practice with children? When will individuals or institutions want to protect their interests? What conclusions can we draw from this?
3   You audiotape an interview in which a teacher who describes what she interprets as inappropriate touching of a number of children by a female colleague. What do you do with this information? What if the co-worker is male?
4   In a survey about teachers' reporting child abuse and neglect, a teacher writes that she knows that the principal at her school is opposed to reporting cases to the child protection authorities or the police because of her prior negative experiences. What do you do with this information?

Further reading

For general information about teachers and child abuse and neglect, see Lowenthal (2001). For a text on early years educational research, see Aubrey *et al.* (2000), particularly Chapter 10 on ethical issues.

References

Abrahams, N., Casey, K. and Daro, D. (1992) Teachers' knowledge, attitudes, and beliefs about child abuse and its prevention, *Child Abuse & Neglect*, 16(2): 229–38.

Aubrey, C., David, T., Godfrey, R. and Thompson, L. (2000) *Early Childhood Educational Research: Issues in Methodology and Ethics*. London: RoutledgeFalmer.

Australian Government Department of Education Science and Training (2003) *National Safe Schools Framework*. Canberra: Commonwealth of Australia.

Bibby, M. (1997) *Ethics and Educational Research*. Coldstream, VIC.: Australian Association for Research in Education.

Brewer, J.D. (1993) Sensitivity as a problem in field research: A study of routine policing in Northern Ireland, in C.M. Renzetti and R.M. Lee (eds) *Researching Sensitive Topics* (pp. 125–45). London: Sage.

Briggs, F. and Hawkins, R. (1997) *Child Protection: A Guide for Teachers and Child Care Professionals*. St Leonards, NSW: Allen & Unwin.

Campbell, H. and Macdonald, S. (1996) Child protection in schools: An evaluation of a training course for Fife schools' co-ordinators of child protection, *Public Health*, 110: 37–40.

Campbell, H. and Wigglesworth, A. (1993) Child protection in schools: a survey of the training needs of Fife school teachers. *Public Health*, 107: 413–19.

Crenshaw, W., Crenshaw, L. and Lichtenberg, J. (1995) When educators confront child abuse: An analysis of the decision to report, *Child Abuse & Neglect*, 19(9): 1095–1113.

Crime and Misconduct Commission (2004) *Protecting Children: An Inquiry into Abuse of Children in Foster Care*. Brisbane: Crime and Misconduct Commission.

Criminal Justice Commission (2000) *Safeguarding Students: Minimising the Risk of Sexual Misconduct by Education Queensland Staff*. Brisbane: Criminal Justice Commission.

David, T. (1993) *Child Protection and Early Years Teachers: Coping with Child Abuse*. Buckingham: Open University Press.

Forde, L. (1999) *Commission of Inquiry into Abuse of Children in Queensland Institutions*. Brisbane: State of Queensland.

Gibbons, J., Gallagher, B., Bell, C. and Gordon, D. (1995) *Development after Physical Abuse in Early Childhood: A Follow-up Study of Children on Protection Registers*. London: HMSO.

Hatch, J.A. (ed.) (1995) *Qualitative Research in Early Childhood Settings*. London: Praeger.

Herzberger, S.D. (1993) The cyclical pattern of child abuse: A study of research methodology, in C. M. Renzetti and R. M. Lee (eds) *Researching Sensitive Topics* (pp. 33–51). London: Sage.

Hewson, D., Nielsen, A. and Powell, C. (1995) Factors affecting the implementation of the NSW Department of School Education child protection curriculum, *Australian Journal of Guidance & Counselling*, 5(1): 99–110.

Hinson, J. and Fossey, R. (2000) Child abuse: What teachers in the '90s know, think, and do, *Journal of Education for Students Placed at Risk*, 5(3): 251–66.

Homan, R. (2002) The principle of assumed consent: The ethics of gate-keeping, in M. McNamee and D. Bridges (eds) *The Ethics of Educational Research* (pp. 23–39). Oxford: Blackwell Publishing.

Hood, S., Mayall, B. and Oliver, S. (eds) (1999) *Critical Issues in Social Research: Power and Prejudice.* Buckingham: Open University Press.

Johnson, R. (2000) *Hands Off! The Disappearance of Touch in the Care of Children.* New York: Peter Lang.

Kenny, M. (2001) Child abuse reporting: Teachers' perceived deterrents, *Child Abuse & Neglect,* 25(1): 81–92.

Kitzinger, J. (1990) Who are you kidding? Children, power and the struggle against sexual abuse, in A. James and A. Prout (eds) *Constructing and Reconstructing Childhood: Contemporary Issues in the Sociological Study of Childhood* (pp. 157–83). London: Falmer Press.

Lee, R.M. and Renzetti, C.M. (1993) The problems of researching sensitive topics, in C.M. Renzetti and R.M. Lee (eds) *Researching Sensitive Topics* (pp. 3–13). London: Sage.

Levin, P.G. (1983) Teachers' perceptions, attitudes, and reporting of child abuse/neglect, *Child Welfare,* 62(1): 14–20.

Lincoln, Y.S. and Guba, E.G. (1985) *Naturalistic Inquiry.* Newbury Park, CA: Sage.

Lowenthal, B. (2001) *Abuse and Neglect: The Educator's Guide to the Identification and Prevention of Child Maltreatment.* Baltimore, MD: Paul H. Brookes Publishing Co.

Miller, K.L., McKeever, P. and Coyte, P. (2003) Recruitment issues in health-care research: The situation in home care, *Health and Social Care in the Community,* 11(1): 111–23.

Miller, W.L. and Crabtree, B.E. (1999) Depth interviewing, in B.E. Crabtree and W.L. Miller (eds) *Doing Qualitative Research* (pp. 89–107). Thousand Oaks, CA: Sage.

Nelson, S. (1998). Time to break professional silences, *Child Abuse Review,* 7(3): 144–53.

New South Wales Commission for Children and Young People (2003) *New South Wales Interagency Guidelines for Child Protection Intervention.* Sydney: NSW Government.

O'Callaghan, P. and Briggs, F. (2003) *Report of the Board of Inquiry into Past Handling of Complaints of Sexual Abuse in the Anglican Church Diocese of Brisbane.* http://www.parliament.qld.gov.au/AnglicanReport.pdf (accessed 15 June 2004).

O'Toole, R., Webster, S.W., O'Toole, A.W. and Lucal, B. (1999) Teachers' recognition and reporting of child abuse: A factorial survey, *Child Abuse & Neglect,* 23(11): 1083–1101.

Patton, M.Q. (1990) *Qualitative Evaluation and Research Methods,* 2nd edn. Newbury Park, CA: Sage.

Pring, R. (2000) *Philosophy of Educational Research.* London: Continuum.

Randolph, M.K. and Gold, C.A. (1994) Child sexual abuse prevention: Evaluation of a teacher training program, *School Psychology Review,* 23(3): 485–95.

Reiniger, A., Robison, E. and McHugh, M. (1995) Mandated training of professionals: A means for improving reporting of suspected child abuse, *Child Abuse & Neglect*, 19(1): 63–9.

Shor, R. (1997) Identification and reporting of maltreated children by teachers in Israel, *Early Child Development and Care*, 134: 61–73.

Sikes, P. (2004) Methodology, procedures and ethical concerns, in C. Opie (ed.) *Doing Educational Research: A Guide to First Time Researchers* (pp. 15–33). London: Sage.

Smyth, K. (1996) An investigation into teachers' knowledge and awareness of child sexual abuse in single sex national schools in Dublin, *Journal of Child Centred Practice*, 3(1): 23–44.

Tite, R. (1993) How teachers define and respond to child abuse: The distinction between theoretical and reportable cases, *Child Abuse & Neglect*, 17(5): 591–603.

Tite, R. (1994) Detecting the symptoms of child abuse: Classroom complications, *Canadian Journal of Education*, 19(1): 1–14.

Van Haeringen, A.R., Dadds, M. and Armstrong, K.L. (1998) The child abuse lottery – will the doctor suspect and report? Physician attitudes towards and reporting of suspected child abuse and neglect, *Child Abuse & Neglect*, 22(3): 159 69.

Volpe, R. (1981) The development and evaluation of a training program for school-based professionals dealing with child abuse: The University of Toronto Interfaculty Child Abuse Prevention Project, *Child Abuse & Neglect*, 5(2): 103–10.

Walkerdine, V. (1999) Violent boys and precocious girls: Regulating childhood at the end of the millennium, *Contemporary Issues in Early Childhood*, 1(1): 3–23.

Walsh, K. (1995) Issues in early childhood teachers' reporting of child abuse and neglect. Unpublished honours thesis, University of Queensland, St Lucia.

Walsh, K.M. (2002) Early childhood teachers and child abuse and neglect: A critical study of their work and knowledge. Unpublished doctoral thesis, Queensland University of Technology, Brisbane.

Walsh, K., Farrell, A., Schweitzer, R. and Bridgstock, R. (2004) *Critical Factors in the Detection and Reporting of Child Abuse and Neglect by Queensland Preschool and Primary Teachers: Implications for Practice*. Brisbane: Queensland University of Technology and the Abused Child Trust.

Watts, V. and Laskey, L. (1993) *Educating teachers in child protection: A right and a responsibility*. Paper presented at the 4th Australasian conference on child abuse and neglect, Brisbane, July.

Wurtele, S.K. and Schmitt, A. (1992) Child care workers' knowledge about reporting suspected child sexual abuse, *Child Abuse & Neglect*, 16(3): 385–90.

7 Restorative research partnerships in Indigenous communities
Jessica Ball

Nothing about us without us

Canada's first peoples hold children's well-being to be key to their social and economic development. The research thrust in Canada in turn is to understand what Indigenous people want for their children and how they can achieve these goals within the broader context of cultural revitalization and capacity building (Mussell *et al*. 2004). However, Indigenous scholars and political leaders in Canada, as in many countries, insist that relationships between researchers (be they Indigenous or not) and Indigenous people must be part of a wider process of decolonization and restorative social justice (Government of Canada 1996). Researchers engaging with Indigenous children are being challenged to rethink the ethics that guide their research, and to establish partnerships with Indigenous groups in order to negotiate the values, conceptual frameworks, methodologies, ownership issues and approaches to disseminating results (Interagency Advisory Panel of Research Ethics 2003). *Nothing about us without us* expresses the principle of participation around which considerations of ethics in research involving Indigenous people in Canada now pivot.

Indeed, the ethics of research involving Indigenous people is one of the most hotly debated issues in research in Canada. Although the number of Indigenous researchers is growing, most research about Indigenous people continues to be done by non-Indigenous researchers, some of whom may be poorly informed about the socio-historical conditions that nearly devastated Indigenous people in Canada (and the government policies that continue to oppress). Researchers may be ill prepared to negotiate research agreements with Indigenous people, to follow cultural protocols and to respond knowledgeably to participants' concerns.

Fortunately, more researchers are becoming aware of the special issues around research with Indigenous people, and their children.

Increasingly, Indigenous communities and organizations are articulating informal or formal written ethical codes of conduct. This is part of a groundswell of activity led primarily by Indigenous scholars to advance new ethics in Indigenous research (Piquemal 2000; Castellano 2004). For example, the National Aboriginal Health Organization, representing First Nations, Metis and Inuit people in Canada, is promoting four criteria for Indigenous research. These are ownership, control, access, and possession at the level of the participating community (Schnarch 2004). The British Columbia Aboriginal Capacity and Research Development Environment programmes, established in many provinces in Canada, has proposed four Rs: respect, relevance, reciprocity and responsibility in research with Aboriginal peoples (BC ACADRE 2004). At the University of Victoria (2004), the graduate programme on Indigenous governance deals with the evolving discourse on Indigenous research ethics and the three guiding principles for research: protection, participation and partnership. These principles raise ethical concerns, such as how to protect confidentiality when data are retained by a community. They also raise practical concerns, for example, the time needed to build relationships and negotiate community-level agreements, and the uncertainty about whether the researcher can count on being able to disseminate results after a project is completed.

One of the three large federal agencies to fund Canadian research, the Social Sciences and Humanities Research Council of Canada, facilitated an intensive online discussion throughout 2003 on Indigenous research ethics (Interagency Advisory Panel on Research Ethics 2003). This forum created an opportunity for Indigenous and non-Indigenous scholars and community leaders such as university-based research ethics board members to come (virtually) to one table to discuss various approaches and to formulate new understandings (Long and LaFrance forthcoming). There was a commitment to supporting self-determination on the part of Indigenous people. The fact that no unified statement or consensus on a specific set of guidelines has yet emerged can be seen as positive, given the current need to stimulate broad local, national and international debate and to bring more Indigenous groups and perspectives into the discussion.

This chapter offers some key learning points derived from ongoing discussions among scholars, as well as a decade of experience in research and training partnerships with Indigenous communities in Canada. The key ethical principle unifying all of the points is *inclusion*, an integral part of a post-colonial, restorative social justice agenda.

- *Learning point.* Non-Indigenous researchers need to acknowledge being members of the dominant culture and being researchers who are in positions of power. The potential to oppress and exploit Indigenous people is a matter of concern, and deliberate efforts should be made to level the playing field in negotiating research relationships.

Never again

Historical conditions of contemporary ethics

Indigenous people have withstood the near destruction of their populations, social structures and cultures. The most catastrophic impacts have occurred through direct physical assaults on Indigenous populations and their ways of life (e.g. germ warfare, raids on Indigenous settlements resulting in the death, capture and confinement of native children and adults, exposure to infectious diseases, and overhunting by traders resulting in widespread starvation). Further depletion of the Indigenous population, their capacity and their resources was effected by the imposition of a land reservation system, which created a system of apartheid and restricted movement of Indigenous people on and off reserves. Their participation in the labour force, education, social programmes, politics and Canadian society as a whole was thereby limited.

For the Indigenous population who survived, a final solution was sought through a government-sponsored programme to apprehend and forcibly confine native children in Indian residential schools (Assembly of First Nations 1994). By 1930, these institutions housed approximately 75 per cent of all First Nations children between 7 and 15 years of age. They were intended to Christianize and 'civilize' the Indigenous population by breaking the bonds between children and their parents, instilling shame about their cultural heritage, and indoctrinating children into Anglo-Canadian values, language, religion and ways of life (Barman 1996). During the 1960s and given the failure of residential schools to break the ties between children and their families, Indigenous cultures began to be acknowledged and governments in several provinces devized a new approach to interdicting the transmission of cultural knowledge and identity from parents to children. Commonly referred to as the 'Sixties Scoop', social workers in the dominant culture were encouraged to apprehend Indigenous children and arrange for their legal adoption into white families (Fournier and Crey 1997). Today, over 40 per cent of all children in government care in British Columbia are Indigenous. In turn, there is still seen to be widespread suspicion of outsider involvement in Indigenous communities (Cole 2002).

- *Learning point.* Researchers who wish to address issues pertaining to Indigenous children need to become familiar with the socio-political history of relationships between Indigenous and non-Indigenous people. The memory and contemporary sequelae of this history continue to influence interactions between Indigenous and non-Indigenous people. Researchers need new forms of interaction to reinstate Indigenous self-determination, to restore power to Indigenous people in their dealings with authorities, and to recognize the rights of Indigenous people to make decisions about involvement in research.

- *Learning point.* Researchers wishing to engage with Indigenous people need to protect the rights of children and their parents or other guardians. Protection goes beyond merely obtaining informed consent. Research procedures should not require isolation of children from their caregivers; they should be fully informed of what will be done with their children and their refusal should be respected.
- *Learning point.* Researchers need to absorb the idea that relationships of trust are the foundation for ethical research practice, and these relationships require unprecedented amounts of time, self-disclosure and care before discussions about research can proceed.

Partnerships

Research is not only about the generation and application of new knowledge. It is also about politically significant social engagement with Indigenous people, based on trust and inclusion.

Some refer to the present as the beginning of a time of healing for Indigenous people (Long and Fox 1996). Researchers have conventionally tended to distance themselves from 'that which is to be discovered'. They have positioned themselves as experts and focused attention unilaterally towards the research 'subjects'. Among Indigenous people in Canada, this unidirectional gaze is no longer tolerated. Rather, researchers who hope to engage with Indigenous people need to be able to account for themselves, for example, by providing details of their ancestry, their family life, their scholarship, and their intentions, not only during initial introductions, but throughout a project.

- *Learning point.* Self-explanation is a first step in relationship-building in research. In order to establish trust, both parties need to define who they are, the scope and nature of their authority over knowledge sources and methodologies, their research purposes, plans and expectations. Cultural literacy is a prerequisite to establishing a partnership with an Indigenous organization or community. Researchers need to observe cultural protocols when approaching an Indigenous organization or community to explore their interest in a research project. Indigenous scholars and community-based agencies are often able to facilitate connections between prospective researchers and groups of interest.

Regaining and retaining control

In an effort to redress the loss of control over their children, social life, means of sustenance, traditional territories and social participation, Indigenous communities are asserting their rights to self-determination, especially in matters concerning their children, their land resources and their culture (Government of Canada 1996). Increasingly, communities that are receptive to research are prepared to articulate the conditions of their involvement in research (see Graham and McDonald 1998; Aurora Research Institute 2002; Akwesasne Research Advisory Committee 2004; Arctic Institute of North America 2004; Mi'kmaq 2004). Often, they seek a negotiated agreement with the lead researcher, as active partners with significant roles in all phases of the research.

To illustrate, a partner in a number of my community university research and training projects over the past several years has been Lil'wat Nation, a rural community of 1600 Salish-speaking, St'at'imc people on Canada's west coast. Their senior administrator there, Sheldon Tetreault, has facilitated discussions with Band Councillors who govern this First Nation, leading to research agreements. Tetreault commented (and signed a consent form agreeing to be quoted):

> We are working hard in Lil'wat Nation to develop our human resources and to create strong programmes for children, and I think that having the interest from the university in what we're doing here is very positive. It holds a mirror up for everyone to see what we're doing, and it amplifies the excitement. We want to retain the staff we have helped to develop and keep qualified people working in our community, and so for them to hear from researchers that other people are interested in what is going on here, and that we are doing things here that can be useful for others to learn from, that's good ... developing long-term relationships, making sure everyone knows what they are agreeing to, and ensuring benefit to the community itself, and not just beyond the community – there is mutuality and respect that I think is exemplary.

- *Learning point.* Negotiated agreements to partner in research involve Indigenous representatives in most activities undertaken by researchers, including: adjudicating the purpose and plans for an investigation; the conduct of the research; accountability of all members of an investigative team; the nature and source of data; data ownership, possession, storage and access; and primary decision-making over research outputs.

Researchers are knowledge brokers with power to collect information and produce meanings which can support or undermine values, practices and people, and to construct legitimating arguments for or against ideas, theories, policies and/or practices. To date, Indigenous populations have been studied exhaustively and their faith in realizing positive returns has all but expired. A frequent comment in communities is: 'Research is a four-letter word around here'.

At a recent conference of the National Aboriginal Health Organization, a First Nations colleague summed up a point made by many participants:

> We are tired of researchers coming in and documenting all the things wrong with our communities: youth suicide, child neglect, alcohol abuse, family violence, poor nutrition, embezzlement. You would think people would want to figure out how we survived white people for so many hundreds of years. How we kept our children alive, kept our stories, kept our knowledge about how to live on the land, kept our ceremonies, kept our fires burning with hope for generations yet to come.

Benefit

Research should make a positive contribution to Indigenous goals. Involvement in research should clearly and directly benefit not only research participants but also members of their Indigenous community (Rheault 2000). Indirect benefits for the 'greater good' are insufficient. In a project on Indigenous fathers, a community member who supported the project for the benefits it could yield for his community asked: 'Why should we contribute to knowledge in Canada? Why should Canadians know about us? I don't call myself a Canadian and neither do lots of people in my community. We will do this [research] for us, but not for them.' After generations of being research subjects while being subjected to racism, many Indigenous people are beyond an altruistic commitment as volunteers in research. One First Nations man introduced himself to me in this way: 'I'm Alphonse, and I come from a long line of research subjects.' He went on to explain that Indigenous people feel they have been 'researched to death, with no benefit to us. Researchers come, they take our stories, take up our time, and leave. We never see any returns from what we gave.'

- *Learning point.* The researcher must be prepared to show specifically how the Indigenous people will benefit substantially within the foreseeable future. Demonstrations of benefit must be conveyed to research participants and possibly to their community as a whole, in terms that are readily understandable and can be directly experienced. A process must be made available for research participants to provide feedback and request changes to research outputs.

Within many funding agencies, Indigenous people serve on review and selection committees and some funding agencies prioritize partnership approaches. For example, the Social Sciences and Humanities Research Council of Canada has a new Community-University Research Alliances programme. The Canadian Institute of Health Institute Research has an Aboriginal Peoples' Health Institute that supports partnership research involving academic institutions and Indigenous communities in Canada, Australia and New Zealand. At the community level as well, leaders often play a major role in vetting research proposals. In general, Indigenous people are demanding assurances of specific and immediate ways in which they will benefit from proposed research.

There is a clear preference among Indigenous groups for research that focuses on strengths of their children and families. Many communities have made enormous strides in their cultural recovery, social organization, and development of infrastructure to support child and family well-being, including health, social and education services, Elder care and cultural centres.

What's ours is still ours, even after we've shared it with researchers

Intellectual property

When Europeans arrived in North America, they claimed to 'discover' new lands. They soon positioned themselves as sovereign over the land and its original inhabitants, casting Indigenous people as subjects. Research involving Indigenous children and families has involved countless replications of this colonialist pattern, including claims to discovery and ownership of knowledge which, in fact, has been passed down through generations. Social scientists have also asserted their singular authority to interpret and represent Indigenous children and families. Indigenous people in Canada have joined global efforts by Indigenous peoples to institute laws governing of ownership, possession and control of Indigenous intellectual property (Couture 1998; Smith 2002). The principles of ownership, control, access and possession asserted by the Canadian National Aboriginal Health Organization are one example (Schnarch 2004).

Ownership

Indigenous knowledge has traditionally been handed down orally across generations through clan and community ceremonies such as the potlatch, pow-wow and puberty rites. Colonial prohibition of traditional ceremonies has meant that much Indigenous knowledge has not been transmitted to younger generations (Couture 1996). Thus, the focus of research is heavily on recording and organizing existing, often ancestral, knowledge, more than on the creation of new knowledge. As holders of traditional knowledge, Elders have a right to ownership of that knowledge, as well as to how and by whom it is transmitted. The source of traditional knowledge must be acknowledged, and permission must be obtained from Elders and their representatives regarding what knowledge can be conveyed to others and in what form.

- *Learning point.* Sources of knowledge (Elders, artefacts, oral histories, etc.) must be acknowledged. Researchers should not assume that participants prefer to remain anonymous. Many Indigenous participants in research prefer to be named, and communities and organizations prefer to be named and credited for contributions to the work.

Possession and access

In Canada, as elsewhere, researchers as well as documentarians (e.g. photographers, journal writers, art historians, and museum archivists) have been keenly interested in dissecting and depicting the lives of Indigenous peoples. Indigenous people are now attempting to reclaim 'artefacts' needed to restore and revitalize living cultures, from collections in universities, municipal, provincial, national and international galleries and storerooms. Most Indigenous communities today are adamant not only about ownership (i.e. clear understanding about who owns the knowledge or the material objects collected – the data) but also about retaining or regaining possession of knowledge or objects of study (i.e. retaining rights to location for storage and distribution). They are equally adamant about retaining decision-making authority over conditions of access.

- *Learning point.* Extreme caution should be taken regarding removal of objects of study from their place in families and communities. This extends to the taking of photographs, removal of test scores, testimonials, stories, children's artwork and so on. Consultation with the Indigenous partner(s) should be sought if removal of information or things belonging to the community is needed for research.

Data retention and storage

Concerns about possession and access extend to data storage. A standard item in ethics protocols at many universities is a declared intention to 'destroy data a specified number of years following the end of the project funding period'. Indigenous community leaders have been distressed at the prospect that valuable information, such as Elders' testimonials, might be treated as so trivial as to be discarded: Elders would be expending precious time and energy in their final years to transmit their knowledge for the research project. A community may request that interview transcripts are stored in the community, for example in a cultural centre, rather than at the research institution, with the intention that these data would never be destroyed. Further, with interviewees' permission, they may wish to attach names of all interviewees to interview transcripts. These data may be of value to the community for their own purposes. Also, many Indigenous people are suffering from 'interview fatigue'. Interviews collected for one project might be useful to provide to a later research project, rather than exhausting people – especially Elders – by asking them to be interviewed yet again. Collection and retention of Indigenous knowledge for continued community use is one way that a research project can 'give back' to the community.

Research methods

In building trust, methods that are readily understandable and transparent are likely to gain more support from partners and prospective participants. Research designs should be short-term or, if carried out over a long period, should include tangible outcomes or reports to partners at regular intervals. Community-based research partners and assistants can advise how individuals can decline to participate or to have their children participate. Indigenous people are less likely to decline to participate if the research has been introduced to them first through a series of events. This might entail announcements in a community newsletter, followed by a community dinner to introduce the research team members and the project, flyers, group forums, and a letter of invitation to individuals. Parents need several opportunities to meet the research team members who will interact with their children, ask questions, and discuss among themselves whether to participate and on what terms.

Participatory research methods, such as participatory action research and community action research, are strongly preferred (Jackson 1993; Reitsma-Street and Brown 2002). Several First Nations organizations have interdicted or disrupted research on children involving certain standardized assessment tools. A few studies are underway to explore the value and feasibility of creating developmental monitoring and screening tools specifically for Indigenous children.

Research methods require active collaboration with Indigenous people who understand their own people and are better positioned to advise on strategies that are informed, respectful and protective. They will be more able than visiting ('outside') researchers to respond helpfully if extra support is needed for participants who are distressed as a result of research participation.

Interpretation

Another lesson learned by Indigenous people is the risk of being misrepresented in research. Nearly every Indigenous community has stories about anthropologists from colonial universities, and before them Indian agents representing the colonial government, leaving their communities and representing their lives inappropriately. Many of these depictions have been steeped in racism and focused only on the negative, helping to justify government-sponsored interventions (Deloria 1995).

Research needs to document strengths fostered within communities, for example: fluency in the heritage language of the community as well as in English; cultural literacy; spiritual values; attention to and memory for oral teachings and observational learning; performance skills for participation in cultural ceremonies; knowledge of the natural environment; and survival skills.

Dissemination

Research outcomes and products must be accepted as indeterminate, with the Indigenous partner making final decisions about what results will be shared within and beyond their community organization, by whom, and in what ways.

- *Learning point.* Reports of results and other products of research to which Indigenous groups have contributed should be presented to them in draft form for editing before any form of distribution and Indigenous partners have the right of veto or censure over research products.

While some might argue that true partnerships do not prejudice the interest of any one partner, it can be argued that, within these collaborative partnerships, the interests of the Indigenous partner organization or community, or of Indigenous peoples as an entity, take precedence over the interests of the researcher and her/his sponsoring organization. An example occurred in one study where findings about the perceptions of Indigenous youth conflicted sharply with findings about the perceptions of Elders in the same community. It was decided to postpone disclosure of the research results until a dialogue within the community could be facilitated by community leaders to explore the intergenerational divergences found. The ethical principle guiding the decision was to seek meaning in the results that would contribute to, rather than disrupt, social cohesion and healing.

- *Learning point.* Researchers must ensure protection of Indigenous participants and communities, including protection from any negative impact that might result from the findings of the project being made public. This may include placing a moratorium on the research for an agreed period of time or keeping data confidential. Co-presenting and co-authoring research reports are widely accepted approaches for disseminating findings. An Indigenous collaborator can discuss the significance and applications of research findings with reference to their intimate personal knowledge of the contexts of culture, community, governance and politics of the subject matter.

Capacity building

Capacity building is a top priority for Indigenous people across Canada. Through partnerships, there is much that non-Indigenous people can learn about themselves as well as about Indigenous ways of knowing, living and communicating. Partnership in research can be an opportunity to learn new skills, explore topics of interest, and network with other individuals and organizations. In my own programme of research, when funding is obtained for research with Indigenous children, Indigenous research personnel are hired at the university and in the partnering communities. Their participation in customized training workshops for the project, attendance at conferences, and opportunities to enrol in post-secondary coursework are a budgeted part of the research plan. In this way, the research aims to contribute to the confidence and capacity of Indigenous partners to offer direction and, ultimately, to assume control of aspects of the project.

- *Learning point.* As part of the collaborative process, the researcher should take responsibility for learning and co-developing research skills with members of the partnering community or organization.

An important aspect of ethical research practice is the choice of values, assumptions and concepts that underlie research questions and methods. Indigenous scholars have been vocal about the need for researchers to consult with Indigenous people about whether the research questions hold meaning, whether plans for carrying out data collection follow cultural protocols and resonate with Indigenous ways of knowing, whether the measurement tools are culturally fair and transparent, and what frames of reference will be used to interpret and communicate results.

- *Learning point.* Indigenous values must be acknowledged by incorporation within the research questions, design, methods, and outputs of the project.

Notwithstanding their diversity, Indigenous cultures in Canada have some commonalities. They tend to be collectivist societies which conceive of individuals as sharing spiritually in the lives of others, both living and deceased. Human life is understood to be an interconnected web of living things and as dependent upon and responsible for the physical environment. Children are experienced as gifts of a Creator, and their lives are understood as spiritual. Children's well-being is seen as embedded in family and community health and wellness across generations. The family, or sometimes the community, is a more culturally fitting unit of analysis than the child alone.

To illustrate, a First Nations Elder explained, in the context of a research study about child-care practices in her community, how concepts that distinguish children according to age, stage or abilities are not meaningful and not wanted in her community:

The idea of early childhood and ideas like disabled children, or that some children have special needs and some children are gifted – these ideas don't come from us. They are not Aboriginal ideas. They come from white people, and from cities. All children have gifts and are gifts from the Creator. We don't like to box people up and separate them out. We've seen how that can be used as a way of getting rid of people, of boxing them up and shipping them out, out of the community to special schools, or what have you. Until we were forced to send our children away to school, we always kept all our children with us, and all together, in families, and we want that again.

Importing research questions, methods, and interpretative frameworks that are predicated on non-Indigenous agendas must be recognized as an intervention that may run counter to the overarching goal of cultural recovery and rebuilding Indigenous ways of family and community life (Stairs and Bernhard with Aboriginal Colleagues 2002).

Summary

This chapter has discussed the ethical principles of respect, inclusion, reciprocity and relevance, contributing towards the realization of a post-colonial research era in Canada. Rather than a unidirectional gaze by non-Indigenous researchers upon native children, a two-way process of mutual learning, sharing and production is considered. It is suggested that negotiated partnership agreements can structure research projects so that Indigenous people are assured of ownership, possession, control and access to data. Partnerships can help to ensure that topics under investigation are priorities for Indigenous people, that they reinforce Indigenous values, are understood using Indigenous frames of reference, and are beneficial to Indigenous people.

Further reading

For further discussion of research in Indigenous communities, see Kirkness and Barnhardt (1991), Letendre and Caine (2004) and Wihak (2004).

Questions for reflection

1   What steps can we take to ensure ethical conduct by researchers and research participants?
2   In cases where we use research methods that evolve over time as a result of extensive collaborative participation, should we offer a continuous process of consent rather than one-off consent at the start of the project? If so, what steps do we take to do so?
3   Does collaboration mean that everyone on a project should share the same goals, values and preferred modes of conducting the project, and agree with the outcomes?
4   Is there a place in Indigenous social research this has been conceptualized in Euro-western academe?
5   How do we acknowledge diversity within Indigenous communities, so that both individual choice and collective choice to participate are respected?

Acknowledgements

Research that enabled the writing of this chapter was supported by grants from Social Development Partnerships Canada (Project no. 9573-10-01.22), the British Columbia Ministry for Children and Family Development through the Human Early Learning Partnership, and the Social Sciences and Humanities Research Council of Canada, Major Collaborative Initiatives Program (Project no. 412-2002-1006). I am grateful to many Indigenous individuals and communities in Southeast Asia and Canada who have taken their time to walk with me on a shared journey of reparation and renewal.

References

Akwesasne Research Advisory Committee (2004) http://www.slic.com/atfe/Prot.htm

Arctic Institute of North America (2004) http://www.ucalgary.ca/AINA/index.html

Assembly of First Nations (1994) *Breaking the Silence: An Interpretation Study of Residential School Impact and Healing as Illustrated by the Stories of First Nations Individuals*. Ottawa: Assembly of First Nations.

Aurora Research Institute (2002) *Doing Research in the Northwest Territories: A Guide for Researchers*. Inuvik, NT: Author.

Barman, J. (1996) Aboriginal education at the crossroads: The legacy of residential schools and the way ahead, in D.A. Long and O.P. Dickason (eds) *Visions of the Heart: Canadian Aboriginal Issues*. Toronto: Harcourt Brace.

British Columbia Aboriginal Capacity and Research Development Environment (ACADRE) (2004) *Research ethics*. http://www.health-sciences.ubc.ca/iah/acadre/site_files/research/ethics.htm

Castellano, M.B. (2004) Ethics of Aboriginal research, *Journal of Aboriginal Health*, 1(1): 98–114.

Cole, P. (2002) Aboriginalizing methodology: considering the canoe, *Qualitative Studies in Education*, 15(4): 447–59.

Couture, J.E. (1996) The role of native Elders: Emergent issues, in D.A. Long and O.P. Dickason (eds) *Visions of the Heart: Canadian Aboriginal Issues*. Toronto: Harcourt Brace.

Couture, J. (1998) Native studies and the academy, in G. Dei, B. Hall and D.G. Rosenberg (eds) *Indigenous Knowledge in Global Context: Multiple Readings of Our World* (pp. 1–14). Toronto: University of Toronto Press.

Deloria, V. (1995) *Red Earth, White Lies*. New York: Scribner.

Fournier, S. and Crey, E. (1997) *Stolen from Our Embrace: The Abduction of First Nations Children and the Restoration of Aboriginal Communities*. Vancouver: Douglas and McIntyre.

Government of Canada (1996) *Report of the Royal Commission on Aboriginal Peoples: Ethical Guidelines for Research*. Ottawa: Author. http://www.ainc-inac.gc.ca/ch/rcap/index.e.html

Graham, A. and McDonald, J. (1998) *Ethical Principles for the Conduct of Research in the North*. Association of Canadian Universities for Northern Studies. http://www.yukoncollege.yk.ca/%7Eagraham/ethics.htm

Interagency Advisory Panel on Research Ethics (2003) Section 6: Research Involving Aboriginal Peoples, In *Tri-council Policy Statement: Ethical Conduct for Research Involving Humans*. Ottawa: Author. http://www.pre.ethics.gc.ca/english/policystatement/section6.cfm

Jackson, T. (1993) A way of working: Participatory research and the Aboriginal movement in Canada, in P. Park, M. Brydon-Miller, B. Hall and T. Jackson (eds) *Voices of Change: Participatory Research in the United States and Canada* (pp. 47–64). Toronto: Ontario Institute for Studies in Education.

Kirkness, V.J and Barnhardt, R. (1991) First Nations and higher education: The four R's – respect, relevance, reciprocity, responsibility. *Journal of American Indian Education*, 30(3), 1–15.

Letendre, A. and Caine, V. (2004) Shifting from reading to questioning: Some thoughts around ethics, research, and Aboriginal People. *Pimatisiwin – A Journal of Aboriginal and Indigenous Community Health*, 2(2), 7–37.

Long, D.A. and Fox, T. (1996) Circles of healing: Illness, healing, and health among Aboriginal people in Canada, in D.A. Long and O.P. Dickason (eds) *Visions of the Heart: Canadian Aboriginal Issues*. Toronto: Harcourt Brace.

Long, D.A. and LaFrance, B. (forthcoming) Truthful dialogue about Aboriginal research issues, *Native Studies Review*, Special Edition.

Mi'kmaq (2004) *Research Principles and Protocols*. http://mcr.uccb.ns.ca/prinpro.html

Mussell, B., Cardiff, K. and White, J. (2004) *The Mental Health and Well-Being of Aboriginal Children and Youth: Guidance For New Approaches and Services*. Chilliwack, BC: Sal'i'shan Institute (info@salishan.ca).

Piquemal, N. (2000) Four principles to guide research with Aboriginals, *Policy Options*, 21(10):.49–51.

Reitsma-Street, M. and Brown, L. (2002) Community action research, in M. O'Meila and K.K. Miley (eds) *Pathways to Power: Readings in Contextual Social Work Practice*. Toronto: Allyn & Bacon.

Rheault, D.I. (2000) *The Ivory Wiigiwaam: Aboriginals and the Academy*. http://www.creatinglearningcommunities.org/book/additional/rheault.htm

Schnarch, B. (2004) Ownership, control, access, and possession (OCAP) or self-determination applied to research: A critical analysis of contemporary First Nations research and some options for First Nations communities, *Journal of Aboriginal Health*, 1(1): 80–95.

Smith, L. Tuhiwai (2002) *Decolonizing Methodologies: Research and Indigenous Peoples*. London: Zed Books. (First published 1999.)

Stairs, A.H. and Bernhard, J.K. with Aboriginal Colleagues and Indigenous

Feedback (2002) Considerations for evaluating 'good care' in Canadian Aboriginal early childhood settings, *McGill Journal of Education*, 37(3): 309–30.

University of Victoria (2004) *Human and Social Development, Indigenous Governance Program*. http://web.uvic.ca/igov/research/

Wihak, C. (2004) Psychologists in Nunavut: A comparison of the principles underlying Inuit Qaujimanituqangit and the Canadian Psychological Association Code of Ethics. *Pimatisiwin – A Journal of Aboriginal and Indigenous Community Health*, 2(1), 29–40.

8 Ethical inclusion of children with disabilities in research
Monica Cuskelly

The World Health Organization (2001) sees disability as an umbrella term for impairments, activity limitations and participation restrictions and as an interaction between attributes of the person and the context in which the person lives. Impairment is a personal attribute, and context may increase or reduce activity limitations and participation restrictions. Despite the acceptance of this definition by more than 190 countries, local terminologies are still often used. Children with disabilities are known as 'children with special needs', and intellectual disability may be known as 'learning disability' or 'mental retardation' in Britain and the United States, respectively.

The two categories (i) people with an intellectual disability and (ii) children are identified by Australia's National Health and Medical Research Council's (NHMRC 1999) ethical guidelines as 'vulnerable populations', meaning that both of these groups are judged to be less able to protect their own interests than are adults (without an intellectual disability). Children with a disability of any kind are not singled out in these guidelines as having particular needs for protection beyond those afforded to all children.

There are a number of ethical issues that researchers face when working with individuals with an intellectual disability, whether children or not. Some of these issues are more troublesome when adults are involved, as the safety net of parental approval may be removed once an individual turns 18 years of age. Some researchers have claimed that the issue of gaining consent from those with an intellectual disability has become so entangled in ethical strangleholds that important research is being hampered (Williamson, cited in Ninemsn News 2004). The challenges around conducting ethical research with individuals with disabilities (particularly intellectual disability) may be seen to be so great as to preclude them from research.

Are the ethical issues we face in researching children with an intellectual disability different from those we face in research with children with other kinds of disabilities (e.g. sensory and physical disabilities)? While there are a number of shared issues, in my view the majority of issues requiring consideration beyond those that apply to research with children generally pertain specifically to those with an intellectual disability. This chapter will canvas both these shared and particular issues, using the term 'children with disabilities' to mean children with disabilities of any kind, and children with an intellectual disability when only this category is intended. Although the focus of the chapter is children with disabilities (sometimes also referred to as children with special needs), some of the research discussed here relates to adults with an intellectual disability as it is relevant to the considerations around children's involvement.

Excluding or including children

Children with disabilities are often excluded from what may be called 'mainstream' research. In some instances this may be entirely appropriate. For example, it may be counterproductive to include children whose language is known to develop differently, such as those with Down's syndrome or those who are deaf (Chapman *et al.* 2002; Blamey 2003), if the research was on the development of some aspect of typical language development in children. In other instances, however, the exclusion of children with disabilities may be the result of a belief that the lives of children with a disability are so different that they should be excluded, or simply of the desire to avoid the additional work that including these children would entail, and that their experiences are of little account when trying to understand the 'big picture'. Most probably it is merely a reflexive response based on the belief that these children can have nothing in common with those who do not have disabilities and, therefore, should be excluded. What does this generally unnoticed exclusion do for our understanding of the diversity of children's experiences?

There is much research that is aimed at understanding some aspect of the impact of disability on children's functioning and/or experience, and in these instances it is necessary to target children with disabilities and their families. In an unexpected twist to the interpretation of inclusion, Connors and Stalker (2003: 27) wrote of their experience of British school principals refusing to send an invitation to participate in research to parents of children with disabilities in their school as they believed research with children with a disability 'was contrary to their policy of inclusion', despite the fact that this research would be conducted at home. This view smacks of paternalism as the principals abrogated the families' right to decide. Further, it reflects an attitude that, if commonly taken up, may lead to the neglect of those with disabilities, and their life situations, in research.

Hallmarks of ethical research

Ethical research with humans has certain hallmarks. Beauchamp and Childress (2001) put forward four ethical principles: beneficence, non-maleficence, autonomy and justice. This means that research should aim to improve the world, should do no harm, should be respectful of the persons involved, including providing sufficient information to make an informed choice about participation, and should ensure that the benefits outweigh the costs. Underpinning all ethical research is the requirement that the research undertaken reflects good research practice. What constitutes good research?

For some time there was contention around the quantitative–qualitative divide. However, much of the heat seems to have disappeared from this argument, with recognition that the research question should determine the research approach, and that complementarities may exist between approaches. In undertaking a review of the literature available to guide ethical decision-making in educational research in particular, Halasa (2000) noted that virtually all such materials were focused on qualitative research. This may reflect the more recent development of this research tradition and the consequent need to translate principles developed for quantitative research into meaningful guidelines for researchers adopting a qualitative approach. Nevertheless, most writing about research neglects any mention of children with disabilities, beyond the platitudinous statement that extra care needs to be taken when researching with those with reduced capacity.

Much more has been written about ethical procedures with respect to children's involvement in medical research than in psychological or educational research. Neither the British nor the Australian associations for educational research offer specific guidance relevant to research with children with disabilities (Australian Association for Research in Education (AARE) 1993; British Educational Research Association (BERA) 2004). The AARE discusses issues relevant to 'socially disadvantaged groups', a description that some writers see as applying to that subgroup of individuals with a disability. Neither of the major international associations dedicated to research with those with an intellectual ability (i.e. the American Association on Mental Retardation and the International Association for the Scientific Study of Intellectual Disability) has statements of ethical research practice to guide their members.

Another question that needs to be raised when considering good scientific research is what the research questions are to be. For a long time researchers working with individuals who have a disability, and with their families, took a pathological view and focused on what was wrong, deviant or deficient in those individuals and their families. There has been a change to this almost universal approach, with some researchers now focusing on strengths and positive family outcomes (see Stainton and Besser 1998;

Muirhead 2002). Some writers argue that research related to issues of disability must be partisan (Zarb 1992). I argue that the biases of researchers (whether positive or negative) need to be made visible in question formulation, data collection and interpretation.

While ethical guidelines may reflect the four aspects identified by Beauchamp and Childress (2001), the specific research issues when working with children are: informed consent, capacity to withdraw, confidentiality and, more recently, participatory research methods, all of which could be considered to be aspects of autonomy. Additional issues to be considered when thinking about children with disabilities these include: intervention research, reluctant families and inducements to participate in research, overcommitment in research projects, and inclusion of children from different cultural backgrounds.

Consent

Australia's guidelines for the ethical conduct of research provided by the NHMRC (1999), for example, require that both children (i.e. those deemed capable of giving consent) and their parents give consent for the child to participate in the research. Some researchers take the position that as parents are the gatekeepers for their children, parents give consent and children assent to their involvement (Connors and Stalker 2003). According to Vitiello (2003: 89), 'Assent is meant to be an explicit, affirmative agreement to participate, not merely absence of objection'. The Royal College of Paediatrics and Child Health Ethics Advisory Committee (2000), however, defines assent as acquiescence, and consent as positive agreement. Whatever the definition, children should give positive agreement to participate in a study before they are included.

The question is whether children understand to what they are consenting or assenting. The assumption of the American Academy of Pediatrics Committee on Drugs (1995) is that children younger than 7 years (or those who are cognitively younger than 7) are incapable of giving assent. In a rare study on children's understanding of the information given to them about a research project and of their own rights, Ondrusek *et al.* (1998) found that Canadian children under 9 years of age had little ability to understand the study to which they had assented. However, Abramovitch *et al.* (1991) found that children were able to understand at an earlier age. Abramovitch *et al.* (1991: 1107) reported that 'almost all seven- to 12-year-olds and a clear majority of the five- to six-year-olds could tell us what the study involved'. According to Ondrusek *et al.* (1998: 158), the studies included in Abramovitch's research were 'psychological studies with very simple designs' rather than medical research which was the focus of Ondrusek *et al.*

No specific methods are available for ensuring that an individual with an intellectual disability is capable of providing consent, and work being done in this area tends to focus on adults (Murphy and Clare 2003). Arscott *et al.* (1998) found that the majority of their sample of individuals with an intellectual disability (age unspecified) were unable to correctly answer the five questions (content, frequency, good and bad things about their involvement, ability to withdraw once consent had been given) designed to ascertain their understanding of a project in which they had consented to participate.

When working with children with an intellectual disability, it is difficult to know their level of ability and understanding until assessment is undertaken. This, in turn, requires consent. The question also arises as to which measure provides the best indicator of capacity – mental age is not always a reliable measure of an individual's ability (Couzens *et al.* 2004), and expressive language and/or receptive language may vary from measured cognitive ability, depending upon the aetiology or cause of the individual's impairment (Hodapp and DesJardin 2002). Certainly aetiology is insufficient in itself to provide anything more than an approximation of ability.

These concerns become even more pressing when dealing with adults with an intellectual disability as parental consent is no longer considered to be an appropriate safeguard. Kellett and Nind (2001) point out that there is a danger in the push for requiring informed consent from all participants as the most vulnerable groups may be neglected in research. As these authors argue, individuals with intellectual disability who are capable of giving informed consent cannot be assumed to be suitable substitutes for those with more severe disabilities.

Several writers have pointed out that judgement about capacity to give consent needs to be made on a project-by-project basis rather than by a blanket decision about an individual's capacity to give consent (see Rosenstein and Miller 2003). Often this suggestion is made when considering individuals with a fluctuating condition, but could apply equally to those with an intellectual disability. Melton and Stanley (1996) note that competence is best conceptualized as an interactive construct and capacity to understand what a study entails and will depend, in part, on the vocabulary used to explain it. The purposes and requirements of some research projects are more easily understood than others as suggested above by Ondrusek *et al.* (1998). Certainly the difficulty of obtaining informed consent does not mean that researchers are excused from the responsibility of explaining the project to children with intellectual disability. As with children under 7 years, however, it may be children's responses to the study's requirements that give a better indication of their willingness to participate.

Abramovitch *et al.* (1991) suggested that obtaining consent from parents before asking the child increased the pressure on the child to agree to participate. While this may be true, no alternative to getting permission from the parent before obtaining consent from the child seems feasible. It is, therefore, the researcher's responsibility to ensure that both parents and children understand that parent consent is not assumed to mean that children will participate and that the child always has the right to refuse.

An additional problem for researchers working with children with an intellectual disability is the tendency of some individuals to acquiesce when asked a question. Matikka and Vesala (1997) found that 11–35 per cent of Finnish adults with mild or moderate intellectual disability showed acquiescence. This has implications both for obtaining consent and for data collection. Researchers need to ensure that questions intended to provide information about an individual's level of understanding of the proposed study are not phrased so that an acquiescent response is taken to indicate understanding.

Consent to participate may require a series of consents (Rodgers 1999), given that it is not always clear at the beginning where the research will end. In a study by Knox *et al.* (2000), at each session there was negotiation between the researcher and participants about the content of the session. While there is no indication of improper pressure in their study, it raises the issue of the potential power imbalance between researcher and participant. If such research were to be conducted with children, even those without a disability, questions would need to be raised about the issue of consent both from children and from their parents who are likely to be excluded from the day-to-day negotiation.

Capacity to withdraw

In the study conducted by Ondrusek *et al.* (1998) most child respondents felt that their parents would react negatively to their withdrawal from the study once they had consented. In addition, most identified that the researcher would be 'disappointed', 'sad', or 'mad' if they withdrew. Abramovitch *et al.* (1991) also found that children felt pressure to continue once assent had been given. Australia's NHMRC (1999) statement specifies that any indication of refusal to participate must be respected.

Vitiello (2003) points out that children may have passing moments of 'frustration and uncooperativeness', and these episodes need not be taken as evidence that assent has been withdrawn. Children with intellectual disability are found to be more likely to exhibit difficult behaviour than are their same age peers (Baker *et al.* 2002; Dekker *et al.* 2002). How does the researcher interpret these signs? Is the child indicating a desire to withdraw, or is their behaviour not specifically related to the research situation?

It could be suggested that parents are the appropriate person to make the decision that the child's behaviour indicates a withdrawal of their willingness to participate. Allmark (2004), however, cautions that parents' beliefs about their rights to determine their child's participation may conflict with the responsibility of the researcher to respect the child's view.

Confidentiality

Confidentiality is a hallmark of ethical research. Some parents may feel their child does not have the right to confidentiality and may want to be privy to their child's responses. In a study conducted by Abramovitch *et al.* (1991) to ascertain children's understanding about research participation, most children did not believe that their responses would be confidential.

Another related concern is the issue of identification of a child as having a disability. Some school-based research, for example, may remove children with learning problems from the classroom in order for them to participate in the study, thus marking them as different. Does this recognition constitute harm (Vaughn and Lyon 1994) or represent a breach of confidentiality?

There is evidence that children with disabilities are more vulnerable to abuse and neglect than are other children (Westcott and Jones 1999; Ryan *et al.* 2001). Disclosures may be made or suspicions raised when working with children with disabilities, and researchers need to consider their likely course of action in such an event.

Participatory research

There is a recognition that the perspectives of children have been missing from the research literature. This recognition is, in part, based on changing constructions of children as participants who are active in shaping their world (James and Prout 1997). This change in perspective has also occurred amongst some researchers working in the area of disability. Some writers recommend more research that seeks the perspectives of children with a disability, where children have the opportunity to speak for themselves (Garth and Aroni 2003).

Proponents of participatory research often go further than arguing for the inclusion of children's participation: they also argue for children's inclusion in the design, execution and interpretation phases. Generally, individuals with an intellectual disability are neglected in these discussions (Kitchen 2000). Nevertheless, there is growing evidence of a participatory approach to research with individuals with an intellectual disability (see Rodgers 1999; Knox *et al.* 2000; Coles 2001), some of which has included children (Fitzgerald and Jobling 2004).

Proponents of the social model of disability (see Siminski 2003) have pointed out that there are benefits for individuals with a disability in the development of a group identity. It is suggested that this group identity gives individuals with a disability more power to change their worlds (Hall 2002). Not all individuals with a disability, however, accept that identity. This may be particularly so for those with an intellectual disability (Craig *et al.* 2002; Cunningham and Glenn 2004). This ethical dilemma is evident in the work of Knox *et al.* (2000) where participants were chosen because they had an intellectual disability, although some rejected this categorization. Should the researcher continue the collaboration without directly addressing this conflict? Does the lack of acceptance by the individual(s) suggest a misunderstanding of the nature of the study and, if so, can they be considered to have given informed consent?

Intervention studies

Children with disabilities are much more likely than are other children to be targeted by intervention research. There are a number of issues that need to be considered with respect to the ethics of intervention research. Some relate to the intervention's potential for harm. Will the intervention, if successful, produce benefits to the individual(s)? Is it well based on theory and/or empirical work? Is the intervention based around the needs of the individual(s)? Other issues relate to the obligations to any comparison group used in the study. Will treatment be offered to all individuals in the comparison group if it is successful? Will the intervention for this group be offered in a timely manner? Finally, researchers need to be conscious of any commercial interests they hold in potential products based on their work and ensure that these interests do not sway their interpretations and reporting of their work.

Inducements

In our own research we are becoming concerned that some families may be choosing to not participate, and that this reluctance is not distributed randomly through the population of children with disabilities but may be strongest in those families whose children are faring worst. This may be based on the challenges of mobility, embarrassment at the level of their child's abilities, or reluctance to see their child perform poorly once again. The problem is that if these children are not included, then the data that are reported paint an unrealistic picture of the capabilities of children with intellectual disability. This unrealistic picture then only serves to convince parents that their child is atypical. Inducements are, of course, only one of the possible ways to address this issue. As indicated earlier, good research is an ethical requirement, and researchers therefore need to be alert to unplanned occurrences that may affect the quality of their research.

Once, it was considered almost unethical to offer incentives to induce possible participants to consent to being involved in research (see Dickert and Grady 1999); however, now it is very common. It is unclear why this change came about – whether recruitment became so difficult that the unthinkable became necessary, or if there was a cultural shift within the research community that suggested that some kind of recompense was right and proper. Some still argue against the use of inducements, although accept that reimbursement of costs is appropriate. Incentives to participate may produce better research as the range of individuals/families prepared to be involved may broaden; however, they may also increase the likelihood that children's wishes about participating in research are given less heed by their parents.

Children who have rare conditions, in particular, may be sought for such a number of studies that their involvement becomes burdensome to them (NHMRC 2002). Parents may not be sensitive to this, or may feel obliged to participate. In these cases researchers themselves must be alert to the imposition and refrain from requesting too much from so few.

Cultural diversity

An issue that is often overlooked in research on children with disabilities in Australia and elsewhere is that of cultural background. There are, of course, many studies that have investigated issues related to intellectual disability from researchers in countries other than Australia. What is rare, however, are studies that examine the role that minority cultural status may play in the experiences and development of children with a disability, including those with an intellectual disability (Ali *et al.* 2001). The invisibility of this group in research means that there is a failure to reflect the diversity of experience of children and to, perhaps, overvalue disability as the most important variable in children's lives, without evidence that it should be given this priority.

Ethical clearance from a research ethics committee does not necessarily ensure ethical research, and ethics committees do not always reflect the concerns of the researched (Newell 1997). Rodgers (1999) discussed a conflict that arose with the ethics committee of her university, although the conflict was between the researcher, who believed adults with an intellectual disability could give their own consent, and the committee's insistence that parents and medical practitioners gave consent for the participant with the intellectual disability.

Strategies for sharing information with children and their families

The traditional way of sharing information with research participants is to write a report at the end of the study. This may be so far removed in time from when the children participated in the data collection phase that they (and sometimes even their parents) have forgotten they were involved. Studies that have checking of data interpretation as an inherent process may reduce this possibility. As one way of keeping families informed we have adopted the practice of writing a newsletter at the end of each year that is sent to all families with a child with an intellectual disability who have been involved in our work. This informal sharing can complement the more formal report that is shared with participating families at the conclusion of the project.

Kellett and Nind (2001) raise the issues of data ownership. This is most relevant to video recordings where the research participant can be identified in the raw data. In our research projects, the video tapes are kept by the researchers in a secure location. Parents know these data are held and that, if they wish, they may have copies of their child's record. In some instances, parents ask for a copy immediately. In other cases, parents may ask for a copy some years later, for example when they are compiling a record of their child's life. In all instances, such requests are honoured; however, once an individual is over 18 years consent for release of the video recording is sought before release.

Summary

Ethical concerns when researching with children with disabilities reflect similar concerns to those raised when researching typically developing children. There are some specific concerns, however, that are related to intervention research and to overcommitment in research studies. It is particularly difficult with children with intellectual disabilities to be confident that procedures for gaining informed consent are adequate because of difficulties in gauging level of understanding, a tendency to acquiesce, and more extreme power differentials.

Further reading

For further discussion regarding research with disabled children, see Beresford (1997), Diesfield (1999) and Riddell *et al.* (1998). For information on gaining informed consent from people with intellectual disabilities, see Iacono and Murray (2003).

Questions for reflection

1. Are the ethical issues in research with children with an intellectual disability different from those that need to be considered in research with adults with an intellectual disability? If so, what additional questions need to be considered?
2. Is participatory research possible with children with an intellectual disability? How might this be developed?
3. What are the consequences of excluding children with disabilities from mainstream research? In which situations do you think it appropriate? When is it not appropriate?
4. Does inclusion imply that those with disabilities should never be distinguished from those without disabilities?
5. How appropriate is it to try to persuade a reluctant participant to continue, or a reluctant family to participate?

References

Abramovitch, R., Freedman, J.L., Thoden, K., and Nikolich, C. (1991) Children's capacity to consent to participation in psychological research: Empirical findings, *Child Development*, 62(5): 1100–9.

Ali, Z., Fazil, Q., Bywatres, P., Wallace, L. and Singh, G. (2001) Disability, ethnicity and childhood: A critical review of research, *Disability & Society*, 16(7): 949–68.

Allmark, P. (2004) The ethics of research with children, *Nurse Researcher*, 10(2): 7–19.

American Academy of Pediatrics Committee on Drugs (1995) Guidelines for the ethical conduct of studies to evaluate drugs in pediatric populations, *Pediatrics*, 95: 286–95.

Arscott, K., Dagnan, D. and Stenfert Kroese, B. (1998) Consent to psychological research by people with an intellectual disability, *Journal of Applied Research in Intellectual Disabilities*, 11: 77–83.

Australian Association for Research in Education (1993) *Code of Ethics*. http://www.aare.edu.au/ethics/ethcfull.htm (accessed 29 May 2004).

Baker, B.L., Blacher, J., Crnic, K.A. and Edelbrock, C. (2002) Behavior problems and parenting stress in families of three-year-old children with and without developmental delays, *American Journal on Mental Retardation*, 107(6): 433–44.

Beauchamp, T. and Childress, J. (2001) *Principles of Biomedical Ethics*. New York: Oxford University Press.

Beresford, B. (1997) *Personal Accounts: Involving Disabled Children in Research*. Norwich: Social Policy Research Unit.

Blamey, P.J. (2003) Development of spoken language by deaf children, in M. Marschark (ed.) *Oxford Handbook of Deaf Studies, Language and Education*. London: Oxford University Press.

British Educational Research Association (2004) *Revised Ethical Guidelines for Educational Research*. Southwell, Notts: BERA. www.bera.au.uk/publications/pdfs/ETHICA1.PDF (accessed 29 May 2004).

Chapman, R.S., Hesketh, L.J. and Kistler, D.J. (2002) Predicting longitudinal change and comprehension in individuals with Down syndrome: Hierarchical linear modeling, *Journal of Speech, Language, and Hearing Research*, 45: 902–15.

Coles, J. (2001) The social model of disability: What does it mean for practice in services for people with learning difficulties? *Disability & Society*, 16(4): 501–10.

Connors, C. and Stalker, K. (2003) *The Views and Experiences of Disabled Children and Their Siblings: A Positive Outlook*. London: Jessica Kingsley.

Couzens, D., Cuskelly, M. and Jobling, A. (2004) The Stanford Binet Fourth Edition and its use with individuals with Down syndrome: Cautions for clinicians, *International Journal of Disability, Development and Education*, 51(1): 39–56.

Craig, J., Craig, F., Withers, P., Hatton, C. and Limb, K. (2002) Identify conflict in people with intellectual disabilities: What role do service-providers play in mediating stigma? *Journal of Applied Research in Intellectual Disabilities*, 15: 61–72.

Cunningham, C. and Glenn, S. (2004) Self-awareness in young adults with Down syndrome: I. Awareness of Down syndrome and disability, *International Journal of Disability, Development and Education*, 51(4).

Dekker, M.C., Koot, H.M., van der Ende, J. and Verhulst, F.C. (2002) Emotional and behavioral problems in children and adolescents with and without intellectual disability, *Journal of Child Psychology and Psychiatry*, 43: 1087–98.

Dickert, N. and Grady, C. (1999) What's the price of a research subject? Approaches to payment for research participation, *New England Journal of Medicine*, 341(3): 198–203.

Diesfield, K. (1999) International ethical safeguards: genetics and people with learning disabilities, *Disability & Society*, 14(1): 21–36.

Fitzgerald, H. and Jobling, A. (2004) Student-centred research: Working with disabled students, in J. Wright, D. MacDonald and L. Burrows (eds) *Critical Inquiry and Problem-Solving in Physical Education*. London: Routledge.

Garth, B. and Aroni, R. (2003) 'I value what you have to say'. Seeking the perspective of children with a disability, not just their parents, *Disability & Society*, 18(5): 561–76.

Halasa, K. (2000) *Annotated Bibliography – Ethics in Educational Research*. http://www.aare.edu.au/indexx.htm (accessed 30 May 2004).

Hall, J.P. (2002) Narrowing the breach: Can disability culture and full educational inclusion be reconciled? *Journal of Disability Policy Studies*, 13(3): 144–52.

Hodapp, R.M. and DesJardin, J.L. (2002) Genetic etiologies of mental retardation: Issues for interventions and interventionists, *Journal of Developmental and Physical Disabilities*, 14: 323–38.

Iacono, T. and Murray, V. (2003) Issues of informed consent in conducting medical research involving people with intellectual disability, *Journal of Applied Research in Intellectual Disabilities*, 16(1): 41–51.

James, A. and Prout, A. (1997) *Constructing and Reconstructing Childhood: Contemporary Issues in the Sociological Study of Childhood*. London: Falmer.

Kellett, M. and Nind, M. (2001) Ethics in quasi-experimental research on people with severe learning disabilities: dilemmas and compromisess, *British Journal of Learning Disabilities*, 29(2): 51–5.

Kitchen, R. (2000) The researched opinions on research: Disabled people and disability research, *Disability & Society*, 15(1): 25–47.

Knox, M., Mok, M. and Parmenter, T. (2000) Working with the experts: Collaborative research with people with an intellectual disability, *Disability & Society*, 15(1): 49–61.

Matikka, L.M. and Vesala, H.T. (1997) Acquiescence in quality-of-life interviews with adults who have mental retardation, *Mental Retardation*, 35(2): 75–82.

Melton, G.B. and Stanley, B.H. (1996) Research involving special populations, in B.H. Stanley, J.E. Sieber and G.B. Melton (eds) *Research Ethics: A Psychological Approach*. Lincoln: University of Nebraska Press.

Muirhead, S (2002) An appreciative inquiry about adults with Down syndrome, in M. Cuskelly, A. Jobling and S. Buckley (eds) *Down Syndrome Across the Lifespan*. London: Whurr Publishers.

Murphy, G.H. and Clare, I.C.H. (2003) Adults' capacity to make legal decisions, in R. Bull and D. Carson (eds) *Handbook of Psychology in Legal Contexts*, 2nd edn (pp. 31–66). Chichester: Wiley.

National Health and Medical Research Council (1999) *National Statement on Ethical Conduct of Research Involving Humans*. www.health.gov.au/nhmrc/issues/researchethics.htm (accessed 16 May 2004).

National Health and Medical Research Council (2002) *Research Ethics Handbook: Commentary on the National Statement.* www.health.gov.au/nhmrc/publications/synopses/e42syn.htm (accessed 20 May 2004).

Newell, C. (1997) Powerful practices: An Australian case study of contested notions of ethical disability research, *Disability & Society*, 12(5): 803–10.

Ninemsn News (2004) *Ethics Hamper Research: Scientist.* http://ninemsn.come.au/Health/story_55611.asp (accessed 23 March 2004).

Ondrusek, N., Abramovitch, R., Pencharz, P. and Koren, G. (1998) Empirical examination of the ability of children to consent to clinical research, *Journal of Medical Ethics*, 24(3): 158–65.

Riddell, S., Wilkinson, H. and Baron, S. (1998) From emancipatory research to focus group: People with learning difficulties and the research process, in P. Clough and L. Barton (eds) *Articulating with Difficulty: Research Voices in Inclusive Education* (pp. 78–95). London: Paul Chapman Publishing.

Rodgers, J. (1999) Trying to get it right: Undertaking research involving people with learning difficulties, *Disability & Society*, 14(4): 421–33.

Rosenstein, D.L. and Miller, F.G. (2003) Ethical considerations in psychopharmacological research involving decisionally impaired subjects, *Psychopharmacology*, 171(1): 92–7.

Royal College of Paediatrics and Child Health Ethics Advisory Committee (2000) Guidelines for the ethical conduct of medical research involving children, *Archives of Childhood Disease*, 82: 177–82.

Ryan, R., Salbenblatt, J., Schiappacasse, J. and Maly, B. (2001) Physician unwitting participation in abuse and neglect of persons with developmental disabilities, *Community Mental Health Journal*, 37(6): 499–509.

Siminski, P. (2003) Patterns of disability and norms of participation through the life course: Empirical support for a social model of disability, *Disability & Society*, 18(6): 707–18.

Stainton, T. and Besser, H. (1998) The positive impact of children with an intellectual disability on the family, *Journal of Intellectual & Developmental Disability*, 23(1): 57–70.

Vaughn, S. and Lyon, G.R. (1994) Ethical considerations when conducting research with students with learning disabilities, in S. Vaughn and C. Bos (eds) *Research Issues in Learning Disabilities: Theory, Methodology, Assessment, and Ethics* (pp. 315–28). New York: Springer-Verlag.

Vitiello, B. (2003) Ethical considerations in psychopharmacological research involving children and adolescents, *Psychopharmacology*, 171(1): 86–91.

Westcott, H.L. and Jones, D.P.H. (1999) Annotation: The abuse of disabled children, *Journal of Child Psychology and Psychiatry*, 40(4): 497–506.

World Health Organization (2001) *International Classification of Functioning, Disability and Health.* Geneva: WHO.

Zarb, G. (1992) On the road to Damascus: First steps towards changing the relations of disability research production, *Disability, Handicap & Society*, 7(2): 125–38.

9 Transforming research ethics: The choices and challenges of researching with children
Glenda MacNaughton and Kylie Smith

Framing research: Taking a transformational stance

Research is replete with choices. In this chapter, we explore the ethical choices and challenges we face in our research *with* young children, rather than *for* and *about* children. These choices and challenges build when we take an ethico-political stance that our research with children should be transformational. It should transform relations of power between researchers and researched and transform relations of inequity and injustice such as those associated with the effects of discourses of gender, culture, ethnicity, class and abilities.

Transformational research has a long history in the educational field where researching with others to produce greater equity and social justice in specific and local contexts is often practised through critically informed collaborative action research (Kemmis and McTaggart 1988; Gruenwald 2003). In collaborative action research, researchers aim to co-research with research participants to transform inequitable and unjust knowledges, structures and practices.

In recent years, our collaborative action research efforts have been aligned conceptually and politically with reconceptualist scholarship that draws from feminist poststructuralist and postcolonial theories of difference, subjectivity, power and knowledge (Campbell and Smith 2001; MacNaughton and Smith 2001).

Principles of transformational research and the politics of research knowledge

Transformational research requires 'the conscious [réfléchie] practice of freedom' (Rabinow 1997: 284) in which researchers consciously and deliberately examine and challenge systems of power and truth that produce inequities and injustices. To consciously practise freedom requires us to generate and use knowledge tactically (Foucault 1980) to destabilize those truths that have inequitable effects and to disrupt to resist their power effects. There is not a simple recipe to follow in doing this, but there are some core ingredients. First, you can destabilize truth by seeking multiple perspectives on your work that challenge your governance by a single perspective (or truth); and second, you can overlay your own truths with marginalized meanings of justice and equity as a way to develop meanings and actions that are more equitable and just. A way to do this is to deliberately seek alternative perspectives on a situation, especially from groups and individuals who experience discrimination and/or marginalization in a specific regime of truth (see MacNaughton 2005). This is a politico-ethical endeavour because it challenges our enslavement to the violence that comes from one view of the world or of a research situation dominating and/or silencing another. As Foucault (1980: 163) contended, knowledge is violence when it silences: 'Knowledge does not slowly detach itself from its empirical roots, the initial needs from which it arose, to become pure speculation subject only to the demands of reason ... Rather, it creates a progressive enslavement to its instinctive violence.'

However, we can contest enslavement and violence by transforming how knowledge is produced and whose knowledge is produced in and through research. Taking Foucault's argument that 'systems of power require some truth to be derived to justify what they seek to do' (Mansfield 2000: 59), researchers are key actors in producing and interrogating the relationships between truth, meaning and power. When researchers consciously interrogate the relationships between truth, meaning and power then the conscious practice of freedom in research becomes a possibility and research becomes the conscious performance of discourses of equity and social justice (MacNaughton 2003).

Performing discourses of equity and social justice requires researchers to be alert to the relations of power produced in and through research. It also requires that researchers seek ways to challenge power relations that have inequitable effects, especially for those groups who have traditionally been marginalized, silenced and/or oppressed in a specific place. This means that researchers need to be consciously ethico-politically engaged in their research processes and outcomes.

To understand this point, it is important to understand that ethics, in Foucault's sense of the term, is not about our duty to act correctly but about the choices we face about how to politically act on ourselves (see MacNaughton 2005). Engaging in an ethico-political process of reflection with others about how we act and practise as researchers enables different choices to be shared and debated.

In this chapter, we share the ethical choices we are making to act politically *with* children in the research process to transform inequitable relations of power between adults and children produced in and through research to engage in dialogue with other researchers about the choices we make. Our interest in researching *with* children links to new images of the child and to a growing concern to include children's perspectives and voices in research (Cannella 1997; Clarke 2000; Woodhead and Faulkner 2000; O'Loughlin 2001) and to our own efforts to co-research with children from within a transformational research stance.

Ethico-political engagement with children

Ethico-political choices

Our conscious ethico-political engagement with young children builds from social justice and equity concerns to protect and enhance children's rights in research with adults. The possibilities to do this in research are several. Three broad tactics that we have used to attempt to protect and enhance children's rights in research with us are seeking to ensure that children have safe spaces in which to share their ideas without challenge or critique, that children's privacy is respected by asking children for permission to document/record what they say, and that children retain ownership of their ideas. We shall now look at each of these tactics further as a prelude to exploring the ethico-political challenges that they bring us as researchers.

Creating safe spaces in which to share ideas and the choice to be a scribe

Children, like adults, are more likely to share their ideas, feelings and perspectives if they feel that those ideas will be treated with respect. To build respectful relationships with children means creating safe spaces in which children have the expectation that they will be listened to carefully and be given the time to think and respond.

Safety also builds for children if they do not feel pressured to express their ideas, feelings and perspectives in one specific way, such as the spoken word. This is especially important when researchers are working with children who speak a different language than they or who come from a different cultural background and context than they. Researchers can use multi-method techniques to support and recognize the diverse ways in which children from diverse contexts might feel most able to share their ideas with researchers (MacNaughton *et al.* 2003). Using multi-method techniques to explore children's perspectives is strongly supported by the work of researchers attempting to develop more participatory approaches to research with young people and children in the Majority World (O'Kane 2000). As Clarke (2000: 3) explains:

These participatory research methods are designed to empower those who take part by enabling people to represent their own situations, to reflect on their experiences and to influence change ... These tools appear to have particular relevance when seeking to reveal the multiple perspectives of young children who are themselves the least powerful individuals in the institutions they are part of.

Furthermore, safety builds for children when they can share their ideas without challenge or critique. If children become used to researchers acting as scribe rather than as commentator or critic of their views then they are more likely to feel safe to share. This is a move that links to what Dahlberg *et al.* (1999: 137), drawing on Foucault, refers to as a 'wider ethical project':

This is part of a wider ethical project of establishing a culture where the children are seen as human beings in their own right, as worth listening to, where we do not impose our own knowledge and categorizations before children have posed their questions and made their own hypotheses.

It also links to children's rights in the research process.

Respecting children's privacy and the choice to extend children's rights

A 'children's rights' approach to research positions a child's right to privacy as equivalent to an adult's right to privacy. Children have as much right to refuse research participation and to refuse permission for their lives and words to be documented as do adults. To enact this position we have to choose ways of working in which children do not feel compelled to share their ideas. Among the questions that we have found it useful to ask ourselves in order to prompt our critical reflections on how to do this are the following:

- Have children agreed willingly to participate in this research? How do I know this?
- What do they understand of what I am doing and why I am doing it?
- Have I created private or individual spaces for children to discuss and agree to participate in this project so that other children don't influence their choice?

In asking these questions the aim is to ask ourselves as researchers how, when and where we will extend the possibilities for children's privacy and their meaningful participation in research decision-making and documentation about them. In turn this links to efforts to ensure children's rights to 'ownership' of their data.

Ensuring children retain ownership of their ideas and the choice to give children data ownership

Who owns research data is a question that arises in all research projects. When children have shared their ideas, feelings and perspectives with us do we have unfettered rights to their use? We would argue that there are clear ethico-political principles that should guide the answer to this question. Children, like adults, should have the right to withdraw data from a research project. Children, like adults, should be able to comment on how their data set is interpreted and presented to others. Children, like adults, should have the research findings reported back to them. Children, like adults, should be part of recording their own data. Emerging research supports children to be part of collecting the data through mediums such as hand-held video recorders, dictaphones and cameras (Giugni 2003).

Ethico-political challenges

Acting as a scribe for children, respecting children's privacy and allowing children ownership of their 'data' each comes with challenges. We now explore these in turn using reflections from our research with young children to open up dialogue about what it means to take a transformational stance as researchers with children.

The challenges of being a scribe: researchers performing research and confirming problematic discourses

In scribing children's ideas, feelings and perspectives, the researcher is giving 'witness' (Lather 2000) to them. Lather argues that giving witness to the ideas, views and perspectives of the marginalized and silenced is a way to be a transformational researcher. However, in working with young children to transform relations of difference between adults and children one is often challenged to 'give witness' to performance of discourses of inequality and injustice in and between children. For instance, in a recent consultation with young children about what makes a kindergarten gender-fair and safe (MacNaughton *et al.* 2004), giving witness to children's ideas, feelings and perspectives meant giving witness without comment or critique to a young boy who did not want girls and boys to play together because:

It won't be fun. Because I don't want to. Because it's not fun. Because we want to play by ourselves and we like shooting the girls because I love guns.

He later said that kindergarten was fair because:

I kill all the girls because I love that.

Should his voice be honoured without comment or critique in these research moments given that, as another boy said, kindergarten was 'fair for the boys, but not for the girls', and that 25 per cent of the girls listed physical harassment by boys as the reason for kindergarten not being fair? In this context, what is performed and confirmed in the research interview when the researcher acts as scribe without comment or critique? Does the research interview become a site in which violent gendered discourses are honoured and confirmed through the silence of the researcher?

Should the boy who sees fairness as being able to kill the girls perform the interview without comment, and should the girls who call for rules to stop such harassment hear only silence in response to their suggestion? Whilst the majority of girls agreed on what was needed to make kindergarten fair, there was no easy consensus on this matter between all the girls and the boys. In his work on consensus and dissensus Lyotard argued that dissensus can create practices of justice: 'Consensus has become an outmoded and suspect value. But justice as a value is neither outmoded nor suspect. We must thus arrive at an idea and practice of justice that is not linked to that of consensus' (Lyotard 1984: 66). What does this mean for researchers acting as scribes for children without comment? Do researchers become suspect by maintaining a consensus between the child as a research participant and the adult as a researcher in which issues of equity and justice are performed without comment or critique? For researchers attempting to take a transformational stance in their research with young children these questions jangle.

The challenges of respecting children's privacy: Adult documentation of the child as a right

Child observation in early childhood education is an everyday practice undertaken by early childhood professionals to assess the child's development (Martin 1999; Curtis and Carter 2000). This practice of adult documentation of the child as a right in early childhood institutions is taken for granted and reinforced without ethical guides in considering children's privacy by accreditation and regulatory requirements of early childhood services (National Childcare Accreditation Council 2001). This form of documentation does not require informed consent by the child and does not provide an opportunity for children to deny or withdraw consent.

If, however, we take a children's rights approach to documentation of the child in early childhood institutions several questions arise, among them the following:

- How do we create a children's rights approach to documentation of the child in early childhood institutions when regulatory bodies require observations? For example, if a child continually refused to consent to being observed there may be no observational records for that child.
- How can we ensure ethical practices of child observation within daily practice in early childhood institutions? For instance, will we do so by asking the child before we observe her, reading what we have written back to the child and then asking if we can keep this information in her records?

These ideas are particularly challenging when researchers are under increasing pressure to produce 'research outcomes' for research funders. How do researchers explain to their funders that their target participants have said 'no'? It is also challenging when early childhood institutions have a long tradition and history of documenting the child without permission.

The challenges of ensuring children retain ownership of their ideas

When you are in the middle of researching with children, the excitement of data unfolding before you can become so enticing you can get caught up in the moment. It is vital, however, to maintain ethical relationships with the child with whom you are researching and continue to gain the child's consent in using her data. The effect of this ethical engagement at times may be difficult because the results can mean that you do not gain permission to use particular data. An example of this is illustrated in an episode Kylie has called 'No. I'll tell you what I like about the room'.

No. I'll tell you what I like about the room

I had been exploring with children aged 3–5 years their identity construction and how 'Barbie' influenced this. I had been working with children individually at the drawing table, documenting their ideas as they spoke. I then asked them to draw and paint the images that they had discussed. I asked children to work individually with me so that they had private space to express their ideas and understandings. Each child waited patiently for a turn throughout the morning. At lunchtime when I had to finish working with the children, Phoebe (aged 4) was waiting for her turn.

She had been waiting her turn since 9 o'clock that morning. I told her that I would come back at 1 o'clock so that we could work together.

When I returned at 1 o'clock I asked Phoebe to tell me what she liked about Barbie. She replied: 'No. I'll tell you what I like about the room.' Phoebe then proceeded to talk about the room and then draw in intricate detail all the objects in the spaces in the room. We spent an hour during which I listened and Phoebe elaborately described the room and what she liked. I frantically documented the words as she wove her ideas together. I had imagined Phoebe as one of the quieter children in the room who spent much of her time in the reflective space reading books. However, her vivid descriptions and elaborate drawings illustrated her interest and interactions in the room in a different light for me. When Phoebe was finished, I excitedly read back her dialogue and pointed out in the painting the issues she raised with me. I then asked if I could use her work to reflect on further and to share with others. She replied: 'Well no. Actually, no I need to take it home.' I replied: 'Oh. Oh, okay, let's put it up to dry and then you can take it home.' Initially I felt deflated. I had been so excited and enticed with the emergence of data that I was analysing it before the ink was even dry. However, on further reflection I became really excited that Phoebe had said 'no' and that I had respected her response and treated her as a competent participant able to articulate her own views and opinions rather than coercing her into giving me what I wanted – her data.

When Phoebe's mother came to collect her that afternoon I explained what had happened. Phoebe's mother asked if I would like her to try to get Phoebe to agree for me to use her work. I said 'no' because if I was to maintain my ethical integrity, Phoebe's trust and respect her right to data ownership then I needed to step away from this piece of data.

This episode sparked two catalytic research moments for Kylie (Campbell 2001). First, Phoebe demonstrated that 4 year old children can understand what it means to consent and/or withdraw consent to participate in research. Second, it highlighted the importance of checking children's consent after data collection. Just asking permission to observe or record what they are doing prior to collection is not enough. As adults would we agree to someone collecting information about us before we knew what information interested them?

Further, this episode left Kylie with several questions:

- How do researchers maintain ethical engagement with children when they are caught up in the moment of emerging data?
- When researching with children, whose agenda takes precedent and why?

- How do we ensure that other children or parents in the guise of supporting the researcher do not coerce children to participate in research?
- How can researchers best consult with children for permission to use data and to ensure that children know what data have been collected?

Final reflections

Seeking children's voices in research comes with ethico-political choices. If we are to honour children we must not only note what they say but also take its politics seriously. With that politics come decisions about how we act with children once we have heard what they say. Inspiration for such action can come from a long line of educators led by Paulo Freire (1970) in calls for education as the 'practice of Freedom':

> the practice of Freedom; the means by which men and women deal critically and creatively with reality and discover how to participate in the transformation of their world. (Freire 1970: 15)

We can draw on these ideas to begin to imagine how seeking young children's voices in and through research might engage us in transformational research for the practice of freedom. It can give researchers a key role in discovering how we can use research with children so that they can 'participate with us in the transformation of their world'. If we care for all children's rights we must listen with care to transform the world with them so that their rights as human beings are honoured in what we do as researchers.

Researchers can also protect and enhance children's rights in research by reflecting critically on how and why they are researching with children. We ask:

- Why am I researching with children as I am?
- In whose interests am I acting?
- Which power relationships (between children and between adults and children) are operating in this research context?
- How can I work towards more equitable power relationships in this research context?

Our challenge as researchers is to find ways to answer these questions in order to retain the ethical rights of young children and enable us to act as transformational researchers.

Summary

Our research choices will produce knowledge that benefits some and works against the interest of others. Our choices will have freedoms and limitations. However, what Foucault argued (cited in Rabinow 1994) was that our choices inevitably expose who we are and who we want to be. Our choices inevitably expose our willingness to search for greater social justice and equity in our work. It is from within these concerns and shifts that this chapter has explored the principles of transformational research with children, and the ethico-political choices and challenges that come from attempting to transform power relations between adults and children in research, especially in terms of informed consent by children.

Further reading

For further discussion on the rights of children in research, see Alderson (2000) and MacNaughton (2003).

Questions for reflection

1 Whose voices are silenced and whose voices are privileged in your research with young children?
2 How is diversity acknowledged and produced in your research with young children?
3 Who has ownership of children's words in your research?
4 How do you report back your research findings to children?
5 What do you see as the challenges in researching for transformation in relations of power between children and adults?

References

Alderson, P. (2000) Children as researchers: The effects of participation rights on research methodology, in P. Christensen and A. James (eds) *Research with Children* (pp. 241–57). London: Falmer Press.

Campbell, S. (2001) A social justice disposition in young children. Unpublished doctoral dissertation, University of Melbourne.

Campbell, S. and Smith, K. (2001) Equity observation and images of fairness in childhood, in G. Cannella and S. Grieshaber (eds) *Embracing Identities in Early Childhood Education: Diversity and Possibilities* (pp. 89–102). New York: Teachers College Press.

Cannella, G.S. (1997) *Deconstructing Early Childhood Education: Social Justice and Revolution*. New York: Peter Lang Publishing.

Clarke, A. (2000) Listening to young children: Perspectives, possibilities and problems. Paper presented to the 10th European Conference on Quality in Early Childhood Education, EECERA Conference, London, 29 August–1 Sept.

Curtis, D. and Carter, M. (2000) *The Art of Awareness: How Observation Can Transform Your Teaching*. St Paul, MN: Redleaf Press.

Dahlberg, G., Moss, P. and Pence, A. (1999) *Beyond Quality in Early Childhood Education and Care: Postmodern Perspectives*. London: Falmer Press.

Foucault, M. (1980) Truth and power, in C. Gordon (ed.) *Power/Knowledge: Selected Interviews and Other Writings 1972–1977. Michel Foucault* (pp. 109–33). Brighton: Harvester Press.

Freire, P. (1970) *Pedagogy of the Oppressed*. London: Penguin.

Giugni, M. (2003) Secret children's business: The black market for identity work. Unpublished honours thesis, University of Western Sydney.

Gruenewald, D. (2003) The best of both worlds: a critical pedagogy of place, *Educational Researcher*, 32(4): 3–12.

Kemmis, S. and McTaggart, R. (1988) *The Action Research Planner*. Geelong, Vic.: Deakin University Press.

Lather, P. (2000) Drawing the line at angels: Working the ruins of feminist ethnography, in E. St. Pierre and W. Pillow (eds) *Working the Ruins: Feminist Poststructuralist Theory and Methods in Education* (pp. 114–29). London: Routledge.

Lyotard, J. (1984) *The Postmodern Condition: A Report on Knowledge*. Minneapolis: University of Minnesota Press.

MacNaughton, G. (2003) Eclipsing voice in research with young children, *Australian Journal of Early Childhood*, 28(1): 36–43.

MacNaughton, G. (2005) *Doing Foucault in Early Childhood Studies*. London: RoutledgeFalmer.

MacNaughton, G. and Smith, K. (2001) Action research, ethics and the risks of practicing freedom for early childhood professionals, *Australian Journal of Early Childhood*, 26(4): 32–8.

MacNaughton, G., Smith, K. and Lawrence, H. (2003) *ACT Children's Strategy: Consulting with Children Birth to Eight Years of Age. Hearing Young Children's Voices*. Children's Services Branch: ACT Department of Education, Youth and Family Services.

MacNaughton, G., Barnes, S. and Dally, S. (2004) *Including Young Children's Voices: A Gender Policy Consultation*. South Australia: Department of Education and Children's Services and the Centre for Equity and Innovation in Early Childhood.

Mansfield, N. (2000) *Subjectivity: Theories of the Self from Freud to Haraway*. Sydney: Allen & Unwin.

Martin, S. (1999) *Take a Look: Observation and Portfolio Assessment in Early Childhood*. Don Mills, Ontario: Addison-Wesley.

National Childcare Accreditation Council (2001) *Quality Improvement and Accreditation System Handbook*. Canberra: National Childcare Accreditation Council (Online). http://www.ncac.gov.au

O'Kane, C. (2000) The development of participatory techniques: Facilitating children's views about decisions which affect them, in P. Christensen and A. James (eds) *Research with Children: Perspectives and Practices* (pp. 136–59). London: Falmer Press.

O'Loughlin, M. (2001) The development of subjectivity in young children: Some theoretical and pedagogical considerations, *Contemporary Issues in Early Childhood*, 2(1): 49–65.

Rabinow, P. (ed.) (1994) *Michel Foucault: Ethics*. London: Penguin.

Rabinow, P. (ed.) (1997) *Michel Foucault: Ethics, Subjectivity and Truth. Essential Works of Foucault 1954–1984. Volume I*. New York: New Press.

Woodhead, M. and Faulkner, J. (2000) Subjects, objects or participants? in P. Christensen and A. James (eds) *Research with Children: Perspectives and Practices* (pp. 9–35). London: Falmer Press.

10 Ethical aspects of power in research with children
Tricia David, Jo Tonkin, Sacha Powell and Ceris Anderson

In this chapter we write as a team drawing from our shared perspectives on the conduct of research with children. We focus particularly on the ethical issues relating to potential power imbalances between the researcher and participants and the challenges of disparity (such as differences in socio-cultural backgrounds, home languages and social mores). While we acknowledge that some laboratory-based child research still takes place, we concentrate on the issue we face as researchers working in real-world settings with children, practitioner-researchers and families. We present a research 'story' from twenty years ago and discuss this in the light of developments in human and children's rights legislation and research sensitivity. The sections in the chapter are led by each of the authors in turn:

- an early research story and reflections on the last twenty years (Tricia);
- seeking sensitive ways to engage young children in research (Sacha);
- reflecting on research contexts (Ceris); and
- developing a research protocol (Jo).

Tricia: An early research story

When I first began work as an academic at Warwick University in the mid-1980s, there was much concern about the difficulties young children in England were experiencing in the transition to primary school. At that time there was a substantial change in admissions practice in the country's schools. In earlier decades, children in much of the country started school at the start of the term in which they turned 5 years old. The move to admit all of the children at the start of the school year, in September, meant that more and more 4-year-olds were to be found in Reception classes (Year R), with teachers who had little or no nursery experience. Familiarizing a whole class of such young children with the school and their base before the long summer break, together with other gentle induction procedures in the September, would be essential.

In collaboration with a local school in a multi-ethnic, multi-linguistic, socio-economically disadvantaged area it was decided that a video would be made about the school. Copy tapes would be loaned to the families of the children being admitted, with the voice-over commentary in relevant minority languages as well as English. In order to decide the video's contents, three focus groups of Year 2 pupils (aged 6 and 7 years) were asked to take me on a tour around the school, and to discuss other ideas they had for filming. The children were asked to think what they would have liked to know, or what a little brother or sister might like to know about the school and school life at the beginning of Year R. As reported at the time (David 1986), this small group of children perceptively came up with the same issues that a large research project (Cleave *et al.* 1982) had published slightly earlier. It was planned that a follow-up phase would focus on the new entrants, exploring the impact (or otherwise) of having had access to the video. (This phase unfortunately never took place because of pressures in other directions in England during the late 1980s.)

Two decades ago, ethical aspects of educational research received scant attention, although clearly it was known that the field of medical research was stringently monitored. Educational researchers, such as those in the field of child development, were expected to 'do no harm'. But it was not until the late 1980s that a growth in the development of awareness about moral dilemmas surrounding educational research instigated the development of ethical guidelines by bodies such as the British Psychological Society and the British Educational Research Association (BERA 2004), like their US counterparts (Aubrey *et al.* 2000). Generally speaking, although the consent of parents would be sought through nursery or school staff, or through direct discussion with parents, no written information would be disseminated, no consent forms distributed and often no feedback given to staff or families. (Clearly the last was not the case in the small project outlined above.) As far as protecting participants was concerned, confidentiality and anonymity were regarded as the main issues a researcher needed to address. Tellingly, children and adults who took part in research before the 1990s were rarely referred to as participants and only a researcher's own sensitivity would ensure participants, especially young children, could express a view about a research intrusion. Often the 'purity' of the methods was seen as paramount, as research about human behaviour was expected to emulate the tenets of science. Other projects during the 1970s and 1980s had, for example, required that I observe and/or interview children at their nurseries, and this too had caused me to reflect on the ways in which they were being treated – ironically being called 'subjects' when in reality they were 'objects' in the research process.

Human rights, children's rights and research sensitivity

Throughout the 1980s and 1990s there was increasing awareness of human rights and, alongside this awareness, of children's rights. The United Nations Convention on the Rights of the Child (UNCRC: United Nations 1989) brought, in its wake, wider recognition of the meaning of child protection. Formerly this term had been used to mean protection from physical and emotional abuse and neglect, and later from sexual abuse, which was gradually becoming acknowledged during that time. Child protection began to take on a wider meaning – commitment to the articles of the UNCRC and to the personhood of children. Later, additional support came from the European Convention on Human Rights (1998), and the renewed Data Protection Act (1998), drawing attention to the difficulties surrounding the collection of data through photography and video recording.

In England, as in many other signatory countries, the British Children Act 1989 (HMSO 1989) was passed, reflecting the principles of the UN Convention, and children's views, wishes and feelings were to be taken into account when decisions were taken about their lives (David 1992). The new Children Act 2004, which received Royal Assent on 15 November 2004, further strengthens the legal imperatives for research. Thus, the legal climate reinforces the increasing moral sensitivity required in research involving children, although it remains the case that it is the parents', rather than the children's, consent for participation that is a legal requirement for this age group.

During the same period, one can place examples of research involving very young children in context, to show the impact of that growing awareness. That is not to say that earlier researchers did not wish to conduct their research ethically and sensitively. Quite the reverse: for many, their decisions and actions were part of the effort to develop greater respect for young children as members of society and as research participants.

In some respects, King's (1984) view that interviewing young children was inadvisable, if not impossible, reflected the assumptions of the time, at least on the part of researchers who were not very familiar with early childhood settings. Such assumptions show an ignorance of the amazing capabilities of young children and indicate the ultimate power of the researcher and the method (no doubt the researcher needed to be seen to be behaving responsibly to the research process and to rigour, no less important now, but only part of the picture). By the late 1990s, other researchers (e.g. Evans and Fuller 1996, 1998) were using operational toy telephones, set up in nurseries, to conduct their research interviews – a method that placed power in the hands of individual children to both terminate the conversation and to talk without pressure from the obvious presence of an adult.

Meanwhile, Elfer and Selleck (1996) raised awareness of how both practitioners and researchers can behave more sensitively with babies, particularly through careful observation. Now, examples of work in progress by new researchers (e.g. Cox 2005; Hawkes 2005) demonstrate their commitment to edging forward appropriate ethical practices. They have been helped in their thinking by the generous, reflective discussions about ethical dilemmas in published studies, such as Pollard and Filer's (1996) case studies of young children starting their primary school careers. Other important contributions to the debates about issues of power in listening to children in research include those of Alderson (1995) and Clark and Moss (2001), the latter being the forerunner to Lancaster (2003).

Sacha: Seeking sensitive ways to engage young children in research

This research account highlights the need for researchers to critically reflect upon their own assumptions, values and aims, the impact of each in shaping the research process, and the potential effects on those who are recruited as participants – with due consideration to age and experience.

As researchers, we must consider how our own experiences in childhood and our practices in adulthood of engaging with young children (as researchers, parents, grandparents, teachers, play-workers, nurses and so forth) contribute to our views about the 'needs', desires, abilities, skills and experiences of young children. How do these 'fit' with the ways in which our society develops rules, laws and subsequent provision for children? How do we construct childhoods as social phenomena? And how, as a result, do we design, conduct and critique our research activities involving young children so that they are sensitive to, and appreciative of, what children may give to and take from their collaboration with us in research?

Of equal importance, however, is the need to take into account the ways in which young children rationalize what happens during the research process in accordance with their own experiences and preferences. Questions remain about the effectiveness of our well-meaning communication with participants, and about how (young) children then deal with information in ways that are meaningful to them, as shown by the following examples.

A colleague visited my children's school and, during the afternoon, discussed with my son (then aged 4) the purposes of the research and my son's willingness to take part. After gaining my son's assent, he 'interviewed' him. As a 'sweetener' for the school, my colleague had taken assembly earlier in the day. When my son returned from school I asked him very generally about his day. The conversation was as follows:

'How was school today?'
'Fine.'

'Did you do anything interesting?'

'I can't remember.'

'Was there anybody new at school today?'

'Oh, a man came.'

'Why did he come?'

'In assembly he told us a silly story about a boy who picked his nose a lot' (much laughter).

'Oh, that's funny (some conversation about the story followed). Did anything else happen?'

'Nah.'

In 2003, I was involved, as a parent, in a large-scale study for which questionnaires were developed. The questionnaires were to be made more user-friendly by the addition of photographs of children, and my colleague asked if she might photograph my own children and some friends. With parental permission gained, two friends came to our home where my colleague explained that she wished to take photos of all four children looking at books together and that the photos would be put onto some letters (questionnaires). These would be sent to teachers in a number of schools, asking them to answer some questions. She showed them an example of the questionnaire, and explained that she thought the photos would make it look much nicer. All four children seemed to understand the purposes of the photo shoot. However, on returning home, the eldest friend (aged 8 years) explained to her mother that she would be famous because her photograph was going to be in the local newspaper again (something that had recently happened to her).

On another occasion, my son came home from school with a letter from a research student seeking parental consent for some research involving my son's class. I explained the contents of the letter to my son, and asked whether or not he wished to be involved (although this was not requested by the student in question). At first, my son said that he didn't want to be involved, although he couldn't or wouldn't explain his reasons. Feeling guilty that I might be letting down a co-researcher, I persisted. Finally, my son explained that he would only be involved if M (his friend) would too, and said that I must check with M's mum whether she was going to sign the letter or not.

My own journey as a researcher working with young children began 8 years ago when I embarked on a doctorate exploring early childhood in China (Powell 2001). At the time, my major dilemmas and challenges seemed to be in relation to data collection, largely at long distance. But I also had concerns about the sensitivities of gathering information, as a foreigner, from Chinese families with whom I had no prior relationship. At the time, I was writing about working within a (then) new paradigm, acknowledging the importance of listening to young children and respecting their views as experts in their own lives (James and Prout 1990), but I was having difficulty enacting these principles that I held dear.

I wrote to the parents of children aged between 2 and 6 years, explaining the aims of the research and the proposed methods. All parents agreed to write diaries and historical accounts as part of the research and to consider meeting me, at a later date, in China, together with their child. In an attempt also to gain the children's consent to collaborate in the research (and be its focus), my communication with parents asked them to discuss the research with their child so that they (and I) might ascertain whether or not the child agreed. It became clear that one inherent difficulty was novelty: neither the children nor their parents had taken part in such activities before, and the children had never met and talked with a foreigner, so explaining and understanding what could or would happen was difficult for all involved.

Subsequently, half of the 12 families who had taken part in the first (documentary) stage of the research volunteered to meet me. Five families appeared to enjoy the meetings, the children were eager to talk, and the parents expressed their pride and excitement about being involved in the study. In one case, however, it was evident at the first (and only) meeting that both mother and child (a boy aged 3 years) were uncomfortable with the whole situation, and the boy barely spoke. My dilemma was whether to foreshorten the discussion or to continue and try sensitively to encourage the boy to talk and express his own views. I made the decision to stop the discussion and to not attempt to coerce the boy to participate. At the time, I was concerned that my evidence from this family was incomplete, but the rationale for stopping the interview was ultimately based on the question 'Am I benefiting this child in any way?' to which the answer was clearly an emphatic 'No!'. Nevertheless, I was anxious that I had not listened to the boy and reported his experiences in his own words. It was only much later that I understood that by stopping the interview I had truly 'listened' to the boy, who had expressed his views through his silence and body language: he simply didn't want to be there!

In spite of having explained the research purposes, and having sought the consent of families, I never really knew anything of what the children had understood and experienced. This was complicated by the context of the research (see the next section). The geographic (and cultural) distance between the participants and myself added to the complexity of ethical issues and of trying to convey the purposes of the research to potential participants.

In an effort to resolve some of these difficulties, some colleagues and I are now engaged in research exploring children's explanations about their experiences as research collaborators, and our intention is to inform the development of approaches to working with young children to ensure that we communicate our aims more effectively and to provide opportunities to generate informed consent.

Ceris: Reflecting on research contexts

My experiences of conducting research with children and young people have taken place outside the academic sphere, mainly through my work as the research manager for a large consultancy practice, where we have undertaken a wide range of studies in the sport and leisure field for both public and private sector clients. As such, I have always taken my steer on research ethics and protocols from the Market Research Society (MRS), the world's largest international membership organization for professional researchers. The MRS sets out clear guidelines for conducting research with children and young people (see http://www.mrs.org.uk/standards/children.htm). These guidelines offer sensible advice in terms of gaining consent, suitable subject matter and specific issues related to the different means of interviewing children and young people.

It is crucial to consider 'context' when planning research with children and young people, for getting simple logistics 'wrong' such as the venue, timing or group dynamics can ruin an otherwise carefully planned research session. Firstly, in terms of venue, it is most important to make the research participants feel comfortable – a 'home from home' environment is the most ideal, although not always possible. It is paramount that the research is conducted in a safe environment and it is advisable that another adult be present. Using facilities within schools can be effective, although again it is important to help participants to feel relaxed and comfortable and it is critical to take into consideration factors such as teacher's time pressures and school politics. At the same time, it is important to recognize the power issues operating in nurseries and schools, where children and their parents might feel they should take part in projects simply because the request comes from those settings. The very nature of being in a school context generally tips the balance of power away from children who are taught to comply with teachers' requests from the moment they arrive. Therefore, it is vital that staff in the nursery or school have a clear grasp of the research requirements at an early stage, to ensure that best use is made of everyone's time.

Some commercial companies and research agencies use viewing facilities to conduct interviews and focus groups as they might with adults. This setting, however, may leave children intimated or frightened by the thought that they are being watched by others, and they may withhold their opinions for fear of 'saying the wrong thing'. Other more extrovert children may see the viewing screens and video cameras as an opportunity to 'perform', and again not be 'themselves' or give their true views.

The importance of making participants feel relaxed should not be underestimated, and it can often be beneficial to carry out research amongst groups of friends either in 'friendship groups', with five or six participants in each group, or in pairs or triads.

Planning the time to hold research sessions with children and young people is also an important factor. For some research, sessions may have to take place after the school day has finished – for young children, in particular, energy levels and concentration can flag quite quickly. Therefore, it is important that the length of each session is planned carefully and the use of stimuli and projective techniques can bring a much needed 'boost' to sessions when energy levels have dropped.

Undertaking research at weekends or in school holidays can often be seen as preferable, particularly if topics need to be discussed at greater length. Obviously recruitment for such a study needs to take place in advance, as this can sometimes present a problem, particularly during the longer holidays.

Other contextual issues to consider might include general 'housekeeping' checks. For example, the researcher might provide light refreshments for discussion group participants, particularly if sessions take place after school. Perhaps even more basic, are simple checks such as ensuring that group members know where the nearest toilets are and that they are able to go before the research commences (or during the research) should they wish to do so.

While such matters can easily be dismissed as 'common sense' and 'obvious', they are often overlooked and I can remember very clearly being involved in a focus group session with four 10-year-old girls, where one member of the group appeared quiet and uncomfortable throughout the session. Following the session, we were concerned and disappointed that we had been unable to engage the girl in the discussions to any great extent. However, it was only afterwards, when we watched the video of the session, that we realized that as she had come into the room, she commented to her friend that she 'really needed to go to the loo', but had not felt able to ask the interviewer at any point where the toilet was and if she could go – a lesson for us all about researcher power!

Jo: Developing a research protocol

The development of a written protocol can be a useful way of resolving and communicating some of the considerations which have already been presented in this chapter. A protocol is similar to the ethical codes provided by research associations. It differs in that it relates to the research dilemmas faced by those researching with children, which a code may not (Morrow and Richards 1996), and is specific to the research project's methodology and approach, and can be communicated to gatekeepers.

In the UK, children inhabit increasingly governed spaces (Prout 2000). Institutions such as nurseries will usually have clearly stated policies on filming and photographing children and on child protection which need to be respected. Large non-government organizations which work with children have formulated policies which govern research with children (Morrow and Richards 1996). A protocol can speak to the concerns articulated in such policies and can go further in reassuring gatekeepers that the rights of individual children will be upheld. It may also reassure if one can point out how the research may benefit the children (Hood *et al.* 1996). Practitioners are not the only gatekeepers. A protocol can be usefully communicated to parents. Attention needs to be paid to the language used. The document should be verbally communicated as well as provided in written form, and questions and concerns invited. Adding logos to a written protocol may add further legitimacy to the research.

However, the motivation for developing protocols cannot simply be about accessing children. When research is being undertaken by a team of researchers, it can establish standards of practice and approach which may not be made explicit otherwise, by the methodology or even in team discussions.

Ethical issues addressed in a protocol might include:

- the research approach;
- why the research is being undertaken;
- the likely impact of the research on children;
- how consent will be sought;
- how differences amongst children will be respected;
- how the research data will be used;
- how children will benefit from the research;
- confidentiality and child protection.

A protocol can also make clear who is accountable for the research and offer parents, practitioners and children a way of raising questions or complaints about the research. (For a list of ten key issues and questions see Alderson 1995; reproduced in Roberts 2000: 229.) A series of questions and topics is also suggested for consideration by managers of UNICEF's Participatory Research and Evaluation (http://www.unicef.org/ evaldatabase). Care must be taken to not focus the protocol unduly on protecting children, although child protection remains a key issue in research with children.

Child protection is a complex and changing area of practice and legislation which may be unfamiliar to researchers. It needs to be seen as a concern which, when addressed through a protocol may bring benefit to both the researcher and the researched. The researcher will benefit from guidance about what to do if a child discloses that they or another child are at risk of harm or when a researcher becomes concerned about a child. The protocol may provide the name of a practitioner, with whom the researchers can share their concern. It can also provide information about what actions should then be taken. Best practice dictates that if a child discloses something which could suggest that they or another child are at risk of harm, the researcher needs to support that child to tell another appropriate adult who will be able to take action (Alderson 1995). This gives the child control over the process and over the way in which information is shared at each stage.

When researching with children who cannot articulate their concerns in speech, the researcher's interpretation may need to be placed in context by speaking to a practitioner. It is important to remember, however, that children's consent for such a sharing is imperative; in some cases, children have been known to disclose to researchers and students because they believed the practitioners in their setting were friends with the adult who was abusing them. It is important not to ignore information gained through communicating with a child or through observation. Child protection is a process of piecing together fragments of information provided from different sources, sometimes over time. Consideration of child protection may also address issues of lone researchers working with a child.

Researchers may be concerned as to how a protocol and addressing child protection, in particular, may interfere with the relationship between the research and the researched. Roberts (2000: 237) gives an example where a disabled young person chose to not talk about their experience of abuse to a researcher who said that they could not maintain confidentiality around issues of child protection. Valentine (1999: 149) argues that researchers need to recognize their moral obligation to the child, even if it means cessation of the research.

Children, power and research

The relatively recent demand for research projects to be scrutinized by research ethics committees and for published reports to include clear explanations about methodological and ethical issues need to be viewed positively, and intended to improve the way we work and the way participants are treated.

Many dilemmas remain and new ones will arise as society becomes more aware of the impact of power relations on children, whether in research or other processes. In this chapter we have touched on some of these issues. Other issues, such as ownership of data, deception, privacy and identification in later life, the membership of research teams and the ability to identify with participants, we leave for readers to consider (see also

Coady 2001).

What needs to be acknowledged is the constant flux of ideas about children, childhoods, research and ethics. Bronfenbrenner (1952: 453) notes that 'the only safe way to avoid violating principles of professional ethics is to refrain from doing social research altogether' (see also Bronfenbrenner 1979). We learn from examining our own and others' mistakes, from reflecting on unspoken assumptions about children and about research. Often it can be the children we know, and who know us best, who can be our most effective 'power-busters', because they will tell us what we may not want to hear.

Thus, there is a need to explore the constructions of early childhood and childhoods and the ways in which our values influence those constructions and our research principles. Becker (1967) asked researchers, 'Whose side are we on?', to which Hammersley (1995) replied that research should be value-relevant.

Some researchers argue that 'childhood, and provision for and practice with children … implies the reassertion of ethical and political dimensions in childhood' (Moss and Petrie 2002: 53). In other words, we cannot escape being political when our work is underpinned by certain values and, as a consequence, certain methodological and ethical approaches. We would argue that, as researchers in the field of early childhood, we have a duty of care to our participants. Tronto (1993) points out that the ethics of care means that we must accept the 'otherness' of the children with whom we work – that is, we should try to engage with the standpoint of our participants but not assume that 'the other' is typical or representative of all.

As researchers, living in the hope of 'pushing back the frontiers of knowledge', we need constant reminders that knowledge production is embedded within our social conditions. As Glenda MacNaughton (2004: 53–4, referring to Foucault 1982) argues:

> Critical theorists reject the idea that meaning, knowledge and, therefore, learning is a uniquely individual, value-free cognitive pursuit. Instead they believe that knowledge and thus learning is always social and always embodies ethics, values and politics. It is always accomplished within a dynamic of power and the specific conditions that produce that dynamic will inevitably produce much of what is constructed and learnt.

Summary

This chapter uses real-life examples of research involving children to examine the ways in which sensitivity to the power imbalances between adult researchers and the children who are participants has increased during the last two decades. Both the researcher's role and aspects of the context are debated, and in the final section suggestions about drawing up an explicit research protocol are presented.

Questions for reflection

1   In what ways would you expect preparation for a research project involving young children to differ from one involving adults?
2   Go back to a research article or report you have read which is concerned with an aspect of young children's lives and/or learning.Note down the key points made about the ethical issues and about power relations within the study. Note the date and location of the research. Do you consider the measures taken and the report adequate in relation to the conduct of research involving young children? If yes, why, or if not, why not? To what extent would you say inadequacies are the result of the era or context in which the project was carried out?

References

Alderson, P. (1995) *Listening to Children: Children. Ethics and Social Research*. London: Barnardo's.

Aubrey, C., David, T., Godfrey, R. and Thompson, L. (2000) *Early Childhood Educational Research*. London: RoutledgeFalmer.

Becker, H.S. (1967) 'Whose side are we on?', *Social Problems*, 14: 239–47.

British Educational Research Association (2004) *Revised Ethical Guidelines for Educational Research*. Southwell, Notts: BERA.

Bronfenbrenner, U. (1952) Principles of professional ethics: Cornell studies in social growth, *American Psychologist*, 7: 452–519.

Bronfenbrenner, U. (1979) *The Ecology of Human Development*. Cambridge, MA: Harvard University Press.

Clark, A. and Moss, P. (2001) *Listening to Young Children: The Mosaic Approach*. London: Coram Family.

Cleave, S., Jowett, S. and Bate, M. (1982) *And So to School*. Windsor: NFER-Nelson.

Coady, M.M. (2001) Ethics in early childhood research, in G. MacNaughton, S.A. Rolfe and I. Siraj-Blatchford (eds) *Doing Early Childhood Research* (pp. 64–72). St Leonards, NSW: Allen & Unwin.

Cox, J. (2005) Is childhood in crisis? Work in progress for PhD thesis, University of Kent/Canterbury Christ Church University College.

David, T. (1986) One picture is worth a thousand words, *Education 3–13*,

14(2): 23–7.

David, T. (1992) Do we have to do this? *Children & Society*, 6: 204–11.

Elfer, P. and Selleck, D. (1996) Building intimacy in relationships with young children in nurseries, *Early Years*, 16(2): 30–4.

Evans, P. and Fuller, M. (1996) Hello, who am I speaking to? Communicating with preschool children in educational settings, *Early Years*, 17(1): 17–20.

Evans, P. and Fuller, M. (1998) Children's perceptions of their nursery education, *International Journal of Early Years Education*, 6(1): 69–74.

Foucault, M. (1982) 'The subject and power afterword', in H.L. Dreyfus and P. Rabinow *Michel Foucault: Beyond Structuralism and Hermeneutics*. Brighton: Harvester Wheatsheaf.

Hammersley, M. (1995) *The Politics of Social Research*. London: Sage.

Hawkes, T. (2005) Promoting development in premature babies: programmes with parents. Work in progress for MPhil, University of Kent/Canterbury Christ Church University College.

Her Majesty's Stationery Office (HMSO) (1989) *Children Act 1989*. London: Queen's Printer of Acts of Parliament.

Hood, S., Kelley, P. and Mayall, B. (1996) Children as research subjects: A risky enterprise, *Children & Society*, 10: 117–28.

James, A. and Prout, A. (eds) (1990) *Constructing and Reconstructing Childhood*. London: Falmer.

King, R. (1984) The man in the Wendy house. Research in infants' schools, in R.G. Burgess (ed.) *The Research Process in Educational Settings: Ten Case Studies* (pp. 117–38). Lewes: Falmer Press.

Lancaster, Y.P. (2003) *Listening to Young Children*. Maidenhead: Open University Press.

MacNaughton, G. (2004) Exploring critical constructivist perspectives on children's learning, in A. Anning, J. Cullen and M. Fleer (eds) *Early Childhood Education: Society and Culture* (pp. 43–56). London: Sage.

Morrow, V. and Richards, M. (1996) The ethics of social research with children: An overview, *Children & Society*, 10: 90–105.

Moss, P. and Petrie, P. (2002) *From Children's Services to Children's Spaces: Public Policy, Children and Childhood*. London: RoutledgeFalmer.

Pollard, A. and Filer, A. (1996) *The Social World of Children's Learning*. London: Cassel.

Powell, S. (2001) Constructions of early childhood in China: A case study of contemporary Shanghai. Unpublished PhD thesis, University of Kent/Canterbury Christ Church University College.

Prout, A. (2000) Children's participation: control and self-realisation in British late modernity, *Children & Society*, 14: 304–15.

Roberts, H. (2000) Listening to children: and hearing them, in P. Christensen and A. James (eds) *Research with Children: Perspectives and*

Practices (pp. 225–40). London: Falmer Press.

Tronto, J. (1993) *Moral Boundaries: A Political Argument for the Ethics of Care.* London: Routledge.

United Nations (UN) (1989) *The United Nations Convention on the Rights of the Child.* New York: United Nations.

Valentine, G. (1999) Being seen and heard? The ethical complexities of working with children and young people at home and at school, *Ethics, Place and Environment,* 2(2): 141–55.

11 Researching communities: Towards beneficence

Collette Tayler, Ann Farrell, Lee Tennent and Carla Patterson

There is growing research interest in the work of integrated, cross-sectoral child and family services within local communities. For several years, the authors have led an interdisciplinary research partnership (in Queensland, Australia) investigating both the mechanisms that underscore effective integrated services and their impact on children, families and communities (Tayler *et al*. 2002, 2004; Farrell *et al*. 2003, 2004). In this chapter we focus on our research within communities to examine the challenges of conducting ethical research that has the capacity to benefit research participants (be they children, parents or service providers) and the communities in which they live. Our work resides broadly within the participatory action research paradigm, seeking to generate and negotiate collaborative relationships between researcher and participants (Aimers 1999; Denzin 2003; Kemmis and McTaggart 2003). Our work could be described as 'applied ethnography' (Chambers 2003: 403) that seeks to improve the quality of the participants' community and family life. We adopt 'a collaborative approach to *inquiry* or *investigation* that provides people with the means to take systematic *action* to resolve specific problems' (Stringer 1996: 15).

We endeavour to reveal the perspectives of various community stakeholders regarding social capital and community capacity in locations where integrated child and family services or hubs are operating. This work includes a pilot study of child, parent, coordinator and service provider views of service provision in urban and rural Queensland and an in-progress study of child and family hubs in a range of urban, regional and rural communities. These hubs, similar in scope to the Early Excellence Centres (EECs) in the UK (Pascal and Bertram 2001) are, however, smaller-scale, community-driven initiatives designed to bring together services to meet the diverse needs of children and families.

The focus of the hubs is the provision of child care and early childhood services, although many include family and parenting support programmes, education and health services and recreational activities (Queensland Department of Communities 2001). The hub initiative was one of a range of strategies designed to encourage communities to play a greater role in local governance, so that ideas, information, and resources from communities become part of the process of policy, programme and service development (Bush *et al.* 2002). The pilot study (2001–2), in partnership with Australia's Commonwealth Department of Family and Community Services, several Queensland government departments and agencies including the Department of Communities, Education Queensland, Queensland Health, the Commission for Children and Young People, and the Crèche and Kindergarten Association of Queensland, investigated two of the first integrated 'Child Care and Family Support Hubs' (known as hubs) to be funded in Queensland. The current study, conducted by the same partnership and funded by the Australian Research Council, is investigating six hubs, with a focus on participants' social capital, sense of community, health and well-being. Such an investigation requires the collaboration of an inter-agency team to achieve the transdisciplinary expertise and focus necessary for analysis of integrated services processes and outcomes.

Beneficence

Our long-term pursuit of this research is testimony to our commitment to improve the health, care and education outcomes of children and families in their communities. As such, our work seeks to adhere to the ethical principle of 'beneficence', that is, the relative merit or benefit of the research (versus the risk) to participants. According to Australia's *National Statement on Ethical Conduct in Research Involving Humans* (the prevailing ethical guidelines to which research such as ours adheres), beneficence denotes the benefits to society as a whole as well as minimization of harm that may flow from the research enterprise (NHMRC 1999: 1.3).

The notion of beneficence in human research has been critiqued by significant international ethicists such as Berglund (1988), McNeill (1993) and Feinberg (1984). McNeill (1993: 167), for example, challenged the inclusive view of beneficence: 'in many of the codes of ethics for research, there is an assumption that the interests of science coincide with the interests of society … However, the assumption is open to question'. McNeill (1993) noted that Hans Jonas, an early philosopher to write on the ethics of human experimentation, questioned the view that science benefits society, claiming that there is often an implicit assumption that the benefits of research are experienced by the whole of society whereas the burdens are suffered by individual subjects or participants. This chapter argues that, while there may be burdens to participants due to their participation in our research, there is an overwhelming case for benefit that may accrue to participants and to the communities in which they live.

Thus, in working towards beneficence, our research into service integration within local communities is underscored by a sustained international thrust to improve access to, and delivery of, services to children and
families (Bertram and Pascal 2001; Connor 2001; Economic Planning
Advisory Committee 1996; Senate Emplyment, Education and Training
Reference Committee 1996; Queensland Department of Communities
2000; Queensland Department of Families 1999; Commonwealth
Department of Family and Community Services 2000). In the United
Kingdom, service integration is central to child and family service initiatives, numerous EECs having been established to 'develop and promote
models of high quality integrated early years services for young children
and families through raising educational standards, increasing opportunities, supporting families, reducing social exclusion, increasing the health of
the nation and reducing child poverty' (Bertram and Pascal 2001: 8). The
evaluation of this initiative indicated that the initial outcomes of the EECs
included enhanced social development, health and reduction of risk for
children, improved parenting skills, confidence and quality of life for
parents, increased skills and professionalism of EEC staff, and the regenera-
tion of communities (Bertram and Pascal 2001). Since that time, England
has increased its effort to integrate services under the wider Sure Start strategy which is planned to extend the reach of integrated services for the
coming decade. Research in Canada and the United States also highlights
positive outcomes for children resulting from involvement in a range of
integrated community services (Connor 2001; Johnson 1993). Despite the
early evidence that integrated service provision directly benefits families
and children, and may also contribute to social capital and sense of community, there remains a paucity of research available to guide and support
this ambitious process.

Social capital and sense of community

Underpinning our research agenda and, indeed, underpinning several government policies towards service integration throughout Australia, is a
growing commitment to strengthening communities through building
family and community social capital and sense of community. Social
capital is attracting worldwide theoretical interest as an umbrella term for
'social networks, the relationships within and between them and the norms
that govern these relationships' (Schuller 2001: 19; see also Baron *et al.*
2000; Schuller *et al.* 2004).

Social capital has been identified in Australia as one of five key
resources used to gauge social and family well-being and functioning
(Zubrick *et al.* 2000) as well as being linked to a range of positive health,
education and social outcomes (Teachman *et al.* 1996; Meier 1999, Baum

et al. 2000; Côté 2001; Lochner *et al.* 2003). With regard to children and youth, increased social capital is seen to help to overcome disadvantage and has been found to be instrumental in improved school retention and general well-being (Runyan *et al.* 1988) and lower rates of delinquency (Wright *et al.* 2001).

Related to social capital, sense of community refers to the feeling of belonging in a group (Osterman 2000). Positive outcomes stemming from a strong sense of community include improved health, well-being, life satisfaction and coping among adults (Prezza *et al.* 2001; S.J. Farrell *et al.* 2004) as well as increased psychological empowerment and collective efficacy (Long and Perkins 2003; Peterson and Reid 2003). For adolescents, benefits have been found to include performance gains at school and lower incidences of isolation and criminal behaviour (Pretty *et al.* 1996; Chipuer 2001), along with a heightened sense of attachment to the community (Pretty *et al.* 2003). The theoretical base, design and measures guiding our current study are derived from these two key constructs, that is, social capital and sense of community. Our research, therefore, takes an inter-agency, cross-sectoral approach to examine social capital and sense of community in young children, families and communities.

Rural communities

In line with Australian government priority areas for national research, our work aims to benefit regional or rural communities, in particular, where service provision can be particularly challenging. In Australia, only 14 per cent of the nation's 20,008,700 inhabitants reside outside major cities or towns (AusStats 2004). Due to the vast size of the continent (7,692,030 square kilometres) this sector of the population often experiences a range of inequities associated with their geographic isolation (Dixon and Welch 2000).

For families living in rural or remote areas of Australia, inaccessibility of services is a key concern. The range of health, care and educational services that are taken for granted in cities simply does not exist in most rural towns in Australia. Lack of access to varied services is a contributing factor to a range of negative outcomes for rural Australians. For instance, compared with their metropolitan counterparts, families living in rural areas have lower income levels, higher rates of welfare dependency (Haberkorn *et al.* 1999), lower education levels and poorer health on a number of indicators (Dixon and Welch 2000).

Not surprisingly, families living in rural communities rate access to health care or advice as a primary concern (Bourke 2000). Lack of access to social or emotional support can also be problematic. Fegan and Bowes (1999) explain that families who are geographically isolated often live a considerable distance from extended family. This isolation also can deprive families of incidental encounters with other children and parents in the local neighbourhood. Research in the United States by Berkman and Syme (1979) highlighted the importance of social support to the health and well-being of individuals. Their study revealed that lack of support from sources such as family, friends, colleagues, the family doctor, community nurse or community organizations was associated with increased rates of mortality.

Rural participants in our pilot research expressed similar concerns about social isolation and the distances involved in accessing even basic services such as a medical practitioner and mobile phone network. Many reported not knowing, or living kilometres from, their nearest neighbour, and they hoped that by becoming a meeting place the new hub would help 'bring the community together'.

Ethical issues

Research with children and families within communities raises a variety of ethical issues. Although our participatory model of action research seeks to recognize local issues and challenges, it is located within a city-based con sortium of government and community agencies and their federation of interests. For more than a decade, action researchers have highlighted the potential for authority structures, particularly in community research, to control the balance of power in the research process (Winter 1987; Hart and Bond 1995; Stringer 1996). We have sought to redress this potential by facilitating more equal access to information and ensuring transparent communication systems, within both the research consortium and the communities with whom we conduct our research.

Valuing participants' informed contributions is essential to promoting ethical research collaborations (Gibbs 1998). This, however, requires a considerable commitment of time to nurture authentic partnerships, especially in isolated communities. As a research team within a large research consortium, we have worked assiduously to develop such partnership. We found that the agendas of our research needed to be negotiated and renegotiated among research partners and community participants, and that we needed to be sufficiently flexible to leave time and space for local communities to register their commitment to becoming involved, and to operationalize their commitment in ways that reflect the history and aspirations of each community. We found that valuing the participants' informed contributions is a critical element in obtaining authentic data for analysis.

Within the research partnership we have worked collaboratively to design, refine and regenerate the ethical protocols, both within our team and within the research communities. In this work we take the role of facilitators working collaboratively to involve the stakeholders in the research process (Aimers 1999). This requires travel to the communities, in some cases involving distances of almost 2000 kilometres from the research base. In the interests of beneficence to the participants and to their communities, we recognize the challenges of the geographic spread of research sites. In order to overcome the tyranny of distance, we devised a methodology for information sharing, using a range of communication technologies, as well as regular face-to-face meetings and mechanisms for incorporating local needs, such as feedback focus groups.

Each community has a local research gatekeeper. We work with the gatekeepers to create the common ground from which to build rapport and trust. This is facilitated by the groundwork of community members who, in most cases, are the driving force behind the establishment of each hub. Our research has benefited considerably from the preliminary work of the local groups who achieved the establishment of a hub in each of their communities. Collaboration with gatekeepers is ongoing and extends beyond the involvement of community members to include the representatives of government in each locality and the local community agencies, organizations and departments that service each hub. Although some of the hubs were operational before our research began, we engage in preliminary and ongoing collaboration with local government and the community agencies in order to engender trust and rapport.

A related ethical issue is the nature of research engagement with communities. Engagement with communities in ways that are respectful of the raft of agendas and interests of our research constituents as well as of the communities themselves is challenging. Research is not merely a process of collecting and disseminating data. Rather, it is a social enterprise, requiring sustained social engagement within communities and their members. A key strategy for ensuring respect was appointing and collaborating with onsite research administrators within each hub community who would work with us collegially to engender trust and synergy within the community. This had added value in contributing to the skills development of the local community and their consequent ability for ongoing and new research activities. Thus, the major thrust of research engagement within our research partnership is to build trust with and among participants. Building trust is essential to conducting ethical research and requires ongoing planning, reflection and negotiation. We have learned to factor in additional time for building rapport and negotiating community support for the research.

A central tenet of trust is respect for participants. To this end, multiple strategies have been devised to ensure that participants are fully informed about the study, the extent of their involvement, their right to withdraw from the study at any time and the confidentiality of their responses. Parent questionnaires, for instance, are accompanied by an information letter outlining, among other things, the purpose of the study and its procedures and an assurance that no participant will be identified by name. Further to this assurance, the original, identified data objects (e.g. completed surveys) are unavailable, except to the small university-based processing team, who subsequently share summarized, deidentified data with the broader research group. In relation to the involvement of children, information letters also describe the nature of children's participation and the types of questions that children may be asked. Parents or guardians are invited to provide informed voluntary consent on behalf of their children, although individual children are also given the opportunity to decline their involvement on the day of data collection.

As researchers we seek to identify our research biases and the potential therein of privileging some data over other available data. Although this cannot easily be demonstrated in any piece of research, a strategy that may test the veracity of different data, and the relative weighting given to certain evidence, is the operation of data-analysis workshops to which transdisciplinary team members are invited to analyse and interrogate the data. In such workshops, original data are reviewed to assess the strength of thematic classifications and to seek alternative explanations or counter-evidence.

Research participants may also take part in a process to provide feedback on their engagement in the research activity. We provide mechanisms for regular feedback, encouraging hub personnel and participants to make direct contact. However, in research of this nature, the ethical protocols surrounding ownership and sharing of data that are designed to protect and safeguard the identity of participants, may well create dilemmas in the event that sensitive data are collected. This requires sustained consultation with community partners so that, in the event of difficult issues arising, there is sufficient trust to deal with issues in a reasonable manner, ensuring processes of natural justice for participants. It is apparent that, in pursuing research with potential to strengthen local communities and individual participants, a more likely outcome is strengthened capacity for both the researcher and the researched. Capacity may include improved research skills, advances in knowledge and strengthened networks with other people and organizations.

Our research design includes regular reports to partners. In the spirit of collaboration and equity, a variety of mechanisms are employed to keep partners informed of every aspect of the study. Given the challenges of busy schedules, partners have negotiated face-to-face meetings only for reporting significant research milestones or outcomes. Day-to-day procedural matters, on the other hand, are dealt with using electronic communication (email, telephone and fax). In addition, a dedicated website is used for the posting of progress reports, outcomes and information to the wider community. This site can also broaden the knowledge base of the group by linking to the dissemination activity of similar groups who are integrating services in other regions and countries.

Thus, in conducting such participatory research, we continue to face the challenges identified by Ghate (2001: 29) in the United Kingdom of 'marrying design requirements to feasibility issues'. According to Ghate, this requires changes to the practice culture, the research culture and the policy culture in which the research is embedded.

Summary

In this chapter we have discussed ethical issues such as pursuing beneficence in transdisciplinary research with children, families and communities. We argue that collaborative research of this kind needs to provide opportunities for generating trust and mutual respect within the research team, the research consortium and the communities in which the research is being conducted. This takes time, negotiation and ongoing opportunities for critical reflection. Beneficence in such research is dependent upon sound levels of trust, respect and openness among research players.

Questions for reflection

1 Consider a piece of collaborative research. What are the features of the research setting, who are the participants and how does the research account for them?
2 What are the potential benefits for participants? How can the benefits be established and measured?
3 What factors might maximize benefits to participants?
4 What factors might limit benefits to participants?

Further reading

To read more on the pragmatics of community research, see Ghate (2001). For further reading on social capital, see Schuller (2001). To learn more about participatory action research, see Wadsworth (2001).

References

Aimers, J. (1999) Using participatory action research in a local government setting, in I. Hughes (ed.) *Action Research Electronic Reader* [online]. University of Sydney. http://www.scu.edu.au/schools/gcm/ar/arr/arrow/aimers.html

AusStats (2004) Australian Social Trends. http://www.abs.gov.au/Ausstats/abs@.nsf/46d1bc47ac9d0c7bca256c47025ff87/d7495af81c170735ca256d39001bc334!OpenDocument

Baron, S., Field, J. and Schuller, T. (eds) (2000) *Social Capital. Critical Perspectives*. Oxford: Oxford University Press.

Baum, F., Palmer, C., Modra, C., Murray, C. and Bush, R. (2000) Families, social capital and health, in I. Winter (ed.) *Social Capital and Public Policy in Australia* (pp. 250–75). Melbourne: Australian Institute of Family Studies.

Berglund, C. (1988) *Ethics for Health Care*. Oxford: Oxford University Press.

Berkman, L.F. and Syme, S.L. (1979) Social networks, host resistance and mortality: A nine-year follow-up of Alameda County residents, *American Journal of Epidemiology*, 109: 186–204.

Bertram, T. and Pascal, C. (2001) *Early Excellence Centre Pilot Program Annual Evaluation Report 2000*. Research Report RR258. Norwich: Department for Education and Employment.

Bourke, L. (2000) Australian rural consumers' perceptions of health issues, *Australian Journal of Rural Health*, 9(1): 1–6.

Bush, R., Dower, J. and Mutch, A. (2002) *Community Capacity Index*. Brisbane: Centre for Primary Health Care, Department of Social and Preventative Medicine, University of Queensland.

Chambers, E. (2003) Applied ethnography, in N. Denzin and Y. Lincoln (eds) *Collecting and Interpreting Qualitative Materials* (pp. 389–418). London: Sage.

Chipuer, H.M. (2001) Dyadic attachments and community connectedness: Links with youth's loneliness experiences, *Journal of Community Psychology*, 29(4): 429–46.

Commonwealth Department of Family and Community Services (2000) *Indicators of Social and Family Functioning*. Canberra: Australian Commonwealth Government.

Connor, S. (2001) *Understanding the Early Years. Early Childhood Development in North York*. Hull, Quebec: Applied Research Branch, Human Resources Development.

Côté, S. (2001) The contribution of human and social capital, *Canadian Journal of Policy Research*, 2(1): 29–36.

Denzin, N. (2003) *Performance Ethnography. Critical Pedagogy and the Politics of Culture*. London: Sage.

Dixon, J. and Welch, N. (2000) Researching the rural–metropolitan health differential using the 'Social Determinants of Health', *Australian Journal of Rural Health*, 8: 254–60.

Economic Planning Advisory Commission (1996) *Future Child Care Provision in Australia*. Canberra: Australian Government Publishing Service.

Farrell, A., Tayler, C. and Tennent, L. (2003) Social capital and early childhood education, *Perspectives on Educational Leadership*, 13(7): 1–2.

Farrell, A., Tayler, C. and Tennent, L. (2004) Building social capital in early childhood education and care: An Australian study, *British Journal of Educational Research*, 30(5): 623–32.

Farrell, S.J., Aubry, T. and Coulombe, D. (2004) Neighborhoods and neighbors: Do they contribute to personal well-being? *Journal of Community Psychology*, 32(1): 9–25.

Fegan, M. and Bowes, J. (1999) Isolation in rural, remote and urban communities, in J.M. Bowes and A. Hayes (eds) *Children, Families, and Communities. Contexts and Consequences* (pp. 115–35). Melbourne: Oxford University Press.

Feinberg, J. (1984) *Harm to Others*. Oxford: Oxford University Press.

Ghate, D. (2001) Community-based evaluations in the UK: Scientific concerns and practical constraints, *Children & Society*, 15: 23–32.

Gibbs, A. (1998) Collaboration between researchers and practitioners, *VISTA*, 4(3).

Haberkorn, G., Hugo, G., Fisher, M. and Aylward, R. (1999) *Country Matters: Social Atlas of Rural and Regional Australia*. Canberra: Commonwealth of Australia, Bureau of Rural Sciences.

Hart, E. and Bond, M. (1995) *Action Research for Health and Social Care: A Guide to Practice*. Buckingham: Open University Press.

Johnson, R.H. (1993) Head Start Demonstration Project: Family Service Centres. Minutes of a conversation hour at the Annual National Head Start Research Conference, Washington, DC, 4–7 November.

Kemmis, S. and McTaggart, R. (2003) Participatory action research, in N. Denzin and Y. Lincoln (eds) *Strategies of Qualitative Inquiry* (pp. 336–96). London: Sage.

Lochner, K.A., Kawachi, I., Brennan, R.T. and Buka, S.L. (2003) Social capital and neighborhood mortality rates in Chicago, *Social Science & Medicine*, 56: 1797–1805.

Long, D.A. and Perkins, D.D. (2003) Confirmatory factor analysis of the Sense of Community Index and development of a brief SCI, *Journal of Community Psychology*, 31(3): 279–96.

McNeill, P.M. (1993) *The Ethics and Politics of Human Experimentation*. Cambridge: Cambridge University Press.

Meier, A. (1999) *Social Capital and School Achievement: Mediating the Effects of Family Structure*. Paper presented at the Annual Meetings of the Population Association of America, New York, March.

National Health and Medical Research Council (NHMRC) (1999) *National Statement on Ethical Conduct in Research Involving Humans.* Available at http://www.nhmrc.gov.au/issues/human/contents.htm

Osterman, K. F. (2000) Students' needs for belonging in the school community, *Review of Educational Research*, 70(3): 323–67.

Pascal, C. and Bertram, T. (2001) *Effective Early Learning: Case Studies in Improvement.* London: Paul Chapman.

Peterson, N.A. and Reid, R.J. (2003) Paths to psychological empowerment in an urban community: Sense of community and citizen participation in substance abuse prevention activities, *Journal of Community Psychology*, 31(1): 25–38.

Pretty, G.M.H., Conroy, C., Dugay, J., Fowler, K. and Williams, D. (1996) Sense of community and its relevance to adolescents of all ages, *Journal of Community Psychology*, 24(4): 365–79.

Pretty, G.H., Chipuer, H.M. and Bramston, P. (2003) Sense of place amongst adolescents and adults in two rural Australian towns: The discriminatory features of place attachment, sense of community and place attachment in relation to place identity, *Journal of Environmental Psychology*, 23: 273–87.

Prezza, M., Amici, M., Roberti, T. and Tedeschi, G. (2001) Sense of community referred to the whole town: Its relations with neighboring, loneliness, life satisfaction, and area of residence, *Journal of Community Psychology*, 29(1): 29–52.

Queensland Department of Communities (2001) *Child Care and Family Support Hub Strategy.* Brisbane: Department of Families.

Queensland Department of Families (1999) *Child Care Strategic Plan 2000–2005.* Brisbane: Department of Families.

Runyan, D.K., Hunter, W.M., Socolar, R. *et al.* (1988) Children who prosper in unfavourable environments: The relationship to social capital, *Pediatrics*, 101(1): 12–18.

Schuller, T. (2001) The complementary roles of human and social capital, *Canadian Journal of Policy Research*, 2(1): 18–24.

Schuller, T., Preston, J., Hammond, C, Brassett-Grundy, A. and Bynner, J. (2004) *The Benefits of Learning. The Impact of Education on Health, Family Life and Social Capital.* London: RoutledgeFalmer.

Senate Employment, Education and Training Reference Committee (1996) *Childhood Matters.* Canberra: Commonwealth Government.

Stringer, E. (1996) *Action Research: A Handbook for Practitioners.* Thousand Oaks, CA: Sage.

Tayler, C., Tennent, L., Farrell, A. and Gahan, D. (2002) Use and integration of early childhood services: Insights from an inner city community, *Journal of Australian Research in Early Childhood Education*, 9(1): 113–23.

Tayler, C., Farrell, A., Tennent, L. and Patterson, C. (2004) Child and family hubs and social capital, *Issues Paper* 3: 1–8. Brisbane: Queensland Government. Commission for Children and Young People.

Teachman, J.D., Paasch, L.K. and Carver, K. (1996) Social capital and dropping out of school early, *Journal of Marriage and the Family*, 58: 773–83.

Wadsworth, Y. (2001) The mirror, the magnifying glass, the compass and the map: Facilitating participatory action research, in P. Reason and H. Bradbury (eds) *Handbook of Action Research* (pp. 420–32). London: Sage.

Winter, R. (1987) *Action Research and the Nature of Social Inquiry: Professional Innovation and Educational Work*. Aldershot: Avebury.

Wright, J.P., Cullen, F.T. and Miller, J.T. (2001) Family social capital and delinquent involvement, *Journal of Criminal Justice*, 29: 1–9.

Zubrick, S.A., Williams, A.A. and Silburn, S.R. (2000) *Indicators of Social and Family Functioning*. Canberra, ACT: Australian Government Department of Family and Community Services.

12 Ethical issues in collaborative research with children
Virginia Morrow

This chapter focuses on my research conducted with children aged between 8 and 16 in English schools. It describes the background to the recent rise of social research with children in the United Kingdom and the development of thinking about ethics in relation to social research with children and draws upon two research projects with children during the late 1990s, one on children's understandings of the concept of 'family', and the other a project that attempted to explore different components of the concept of 'social capital' with children. The chapter examines issues related to gaining a sample of participants and consent, describes an ethical dilemma, and briefly raises challenges for researchers around taking forward research with children.

During the 1990s there was an increase in the demand for children's views and opinions to be sought in matters that affect them. The UK government ratified the United Nations Convention on the Rights of the Child (UNCRC) in 1991. The UNCRC acknowledges that children have the right to be consulted and taken account of, to have access to information, to freedom of speech and opinion, and to challenge decisions made on their behalf. If this set of principles was respected, it would clearly represent a major shift in the recognition of children as participants in society (Lansdown 1994). In 1994, the International Year of the Family (IYF) Agenda for Action highlighted the issue of strengthening children's rights and incorporating children's views 'when decisions are made about them in their families and at school' (IYF 1994: 10). In law, the Children Act 1989 (HMSO 1989) stipulated that courts shall have particular regard to 'the ascertainable wishes and feelings of the child concerned (considered in the light of his [sic] age and understanding)' (Section 1(3)(a)). Correspondingly, in some areas of social research there was growing recognition that children's perspectives can and should be elicited on a range of issues that affect them. As Boyden and Ennew (1997: 10) note:

> It is evident that there is a pressing need for appropriate and well planned research with children, both pure and applied ... research

about children's lives is also essential if policies and programmes are to become more responsive and relevant to their concerns and needs. More important still is to find ways of doing research with children that provide valid, good quality information and also protect them from processes that fail to respect their ideas and integrity, exploit them or intrude into their privacy.

During the late 1990s, the UK's Economic and Social Research Council funded a research programme, *Children 5-16*, that consisted of 20 projects, completed in 2002.

When I began my research career in 1988, however, there was little published material that referred to carrying out research with children as 'informants'. Rarely were children mentioned in research methods text-books. There was information about qualitative research in educational settings, but the sociology of education is not 'about' children – though this is changing with projects on 'pupil voice' (see Ruddock and Flutter 2004). Similarly, there was material on researching the sociology of the family – but again, this was not 'about children', and we knew little about children's experiences of family life, which is all the more surprising given that, to a significant extent, children can be said to constitute families; this has also changed (see Brannen and O'Brien 1996; Smart *et al.* 2001). Both the sociology of the family and the sociology of education had tended to use adults – parents or teachers – as proxy informants about children. It was in this vacuum that I undertook to explore children's conceptualizations of family (Morrow 1998a), the first task of which involved addressing and exploring the ethics of the research (Morrow and Richards 1996). At the same time Alderson (1995) published a seminal guide to ethics in research with children (see also Alderson and Morrow 2004). I turn now to a brief discussion of the main differences between adults and children in social research.

Thinking ethically about children

Questions about ethics of research with children can, to an extent, be reduced to how far children are regarded as similar to or different from adults. These discussions, in turn, can be reduced to two related descriptive perceptions that adults hold of children, that is, children as vulnerable and children as incompetent. These conceptualizations are reinforced by legal notions of childhood as a period of powerlessness and irresponsibility.

'Vulnerable' children

Previous published work on the ethics of research with children had been dominated by discussions of the ethical dilemmas raised by medical and psychological research (see Nicholson 1986; Stanley and Sieber 1992; Grodin and Glantz 1994). However, such discussions were dominated by a conceptualization of children as vulnerable and in need of protection from exploitative researchers, and as *objects* rather than subjects of research. In other words, the methodological starting points for such discussions, and the epistemological assumptions about what children are like, were based on a specific formulation of the category 'child'. This formulation needs to be examined critically if we are to attempt a *social* analysis of children's experiences, and, in so doing, are to see children as social actors in their own right.

Second, not least for funding reasons and the drive for social research to be 'policy-relevant', research with children in UK tended to be domi-nated by concerns about groups of children who are vulnerable in some way, whose vulnerability is seen to be problematic (Qvortrup 1987). Again a specific conceptualization of children appeared to dominate, that of chil-dren as weak, passive and open to abuse. Research tended to focus on chil-dren already damaged by their experiences. Rightly, these children were seen as in need of protection from further harm by researchers who may cause distress by asking children to describe adverse experiences. The con-sequence of this, however, was that we knew something about certain prob-lematic groups of children, and very little at all about 'ordinary' children, and we had no background, contextual or baseline information with which to compare the experiences of vulnerable children with others.

Lansdown (1994) suggested that children are vulnerable in two respects. First, they are inherently vulnerable because of their physical dependency upon the adults around them. Second, they are structurally vulnerable, 'because of their total lack of political and economic power and their lack of civil rights' (Landsdown 1994: 35), which derives from histor-ical attitudes and presumptions about the nature of childhood. She empha-sizes that

> there is a tendency to rely too heavily on a presumption of chil-dren's biological and psychological vulnerability in developing our law, policy and practice, and insufficient focus on the extent to which their lack of civil status creates that vulnerability. (Landsdown 1994: 35)

The consequence of this presented a dilemma for social researchers: we simply were not used to talking to children to try to ascertain their views and opinions.

Third, the perceived vulnerability of children means that the obliga-tions, duties and responsibilities of researchers towards research subjects are qualitatively different when working with children, and relate to adult responsibilities towards children in general. Thus, if a child discloses that he or she is at risk of harm, then the assumption is that the researcher has a duty to pass this information on to a professional who can protect the child/other children at risk. Researchers have moral obligations as adults to protect children at risk even when this may mean losing access to, or the trust of, the children concerned if they do intervene. On the other hand, children expect adults to behave in certain ways, and by not intervening in certain situations adult researchers may lose credibility (Boyden and Ennew 1997). Depending on the context, nature of the disclosure, age of the child, relationship of child to researcher, most guidance suggests that the researcher should try to discuss with the child what strategy they would like to pursue (Butler and Williamson 1994; Alderson and Morrow 2004). Similarly, researchers who come across adults who may be at risk in some way should also try to find strategies for supporting a vulnerable adult. However, there must always be a danger of the research drawing attention to problematic situations which the child did not perceive as a problem in the first place.

'Incompetent' children

The other key perceived difference between children and adults in research that dominated for many years was children's assumed lack of competence: competence to make decisions about whether to participate in research, and competence to provide valid sociological data. Alderson (1993) has been central in shifting this conceptualization – and researchers now accept that children's competence to participate in decision-making arises through a combination of experience and relationships, and should not necessarily be seen as age-related. Conceptualizing children as less competent provided teachers and parents (and sociologists) with powerful normative models for what children are (or should be) like, and it remains the dominant paradigm in the training of professionals working with children. It reflects a cultural reluctance to take children's ideas seriously, which in itself is not surprising, given that, at the macro-social level at any rate, adults have tended to trivialize and devalue children's acts as a matter of course (see Waksler 1991).

Powerless children

A major challenge for researchers working with children lies in the disparities in power and status between adults and children. Mayall (1994) argues that data collection with children offers focusses on children's capacities to give truthful accounts, childrens experience and knowledge and the social construction of their accounts.

She notes that these also apply to research with adults. For Mayall (1994), the differential power relationship between children and adults in the research process lies at the level of interpretation of data, rather that at the point of data collection; she suggests that whatever the data collection method,

> ... in considering data, the presentation of it is likely to require analysis and interpretations, at least for some purposes, which do demand different knowledge than that generally available to children, in order to explicate children's social status and structural positioning. (Mayall 1994: 11)

James *et al.* (1998) suggest that ways of 'seeing children' have a profound impact upon the way in which we study children. Here, too, the power to choose the standpoint or way of seeing lies with the researcher. The methods we use, the research populations and subjects we study and, crucially, the interpretation of the data collected, are influenced by our view of children (see Mayall 2002 for a 'child standpoint').

Methodologically, researchers need to consider the standpoint from which they research children, and the ethical implications of that standpoint. This involves respecting children's competences. Indeed, respect needs to become a methodological technique in itself, and researchers need to set aside 'natural' adult tendencies 'both to take children for granted and to accord them a provisional status ... The belief that children are inherently "wrong" when they disagree with adults is an obstacle to be overcome' (Fine and Sandstrom 1988: 75–6).

Interactive and participatory research methods may be useful in research with children (see Ennew 1994; Johnson *et al.* 1995). It is also possible to use children as research assistants and data collectors (Alderson 2000; Kellett *et al.* 2004). Using non-invasive, non-confrontational methods may also help to avoid 'undue intrusion' and diminish power imbalances.

One way to address the power imbalance in interpretation of data is to return to research respondents and ask for their input into the analysis of the data. Research respondents have to be willing for this to happen, but often the time delay between data collection and writing up, plus problems of access to children, may discourage researchers from doing so.

Finally, at the stage of dissemination of research findings, the potential for journalists or policy specialists to sensationalize issues may be great. Researchers must bear responsibility for how children are represented in reports of research in the media (Boyden and Ennew 1997). Children, as a powerless group, are not able to challenge the ways in which research findings about them are presented. A further point is that discussions about ethics in social research in general tend to focus on qualitative methods as having the potential for most intrusion and hence are the most ethically precarious, but survey methods also carry the potential for harm, particularly at the level of dissemination where again children may be misrepresented in sensationalized accounts.

The next section describes some examples from my research, and focuses on research ethics – seeking consent, children's views on being involved in research, and reporting back to children.

Project 1: Children's views on 'having a say in decisions'

Project 1 was a research project that explored children's understandings of family, with 184 children aged between 8 and 14 years in rural and urban schools. Data were collected in 1996 and 1997. A proportion of the urban sample (*n* = 52) were Muslim children of Pakistani Mirpuri origin. The rationale for selecting these samples was related to the overall aims of the project, one of which was to explore stereotypical assumptions about kinship and family with a minority ethnic group assumed to be very different from the majority culture. The research also aimed to redress an imbalance in that the experiences and perspectives of children from minority ethnic groups are underrepresented in social research. The samples were selected to reflect age and gender differences, and schools were chosen because their composition reflected a range of socio-economic circumstances. The research used a number of qualitative data-collection techniques, including drawing, written work in the form of sentence completion and descriptions of who is important, and group discussions on a range of topics including media images of families, children's rights and 'being listened to' (see Morrow 1998a, b, 1999a, b, 2002).

The research explored norms, values and representations, and children's ideas and use of language in talking about 'family', and did not focus on individual personal experiences and family backgrounds. The research explored the defining characteristics of 'family' from children's perspectives and, given that 'children' are not a homogenous group, to find out whether there were differences in these definitions related to gender, age, and ethnic or religious background. The project was approved by my local (university) psychology research ethics committee (who requested to see the information letter for parents).

Project 2: Children and 'social capital'

Project 2 consisted of a research project conducted for the Health Education Authority (HEA, the health promotion arm of the Department of Health, now the Health Development Agency) that explored the relevance of Putnam's (1993) concept of 'social capital' in relation to children. 'Social capital' was defined as consisting of: social and community networks; civic engagement or participation; community identity and sense of belonging; and norms of cooperation, reciprocity and trust of others within the community (Putnam 1993). The premise is that levels of 'social capital' in a community have an important effect on people's well-being. 'Social capital' is a notion that has been contested at a number of levels, conceptually, methodologically and theoretically (discussed elsewhere, see Morrow 1999a, 2001a, b).

The research was conducted in two schools in relatively deprived wards in a town in South-East England (disguised as 'Springtown'; children chose their own pseudonyms and the site was chosen to match another HEA study on adults and social capital). The sample comprised 101 boys and girls in two age bands: 12–13-year-olds and 14–15-year-olds, with a significant proportion from minority ethnic groups. The project used a combination of qualitative research methods and structured activities (including photography using disposable cameras, map drawing, descriptions of who is important, activities outside school, and group discussions) to explore young people's subjective experiences of their neighbourhoods, the nature of their social networks, and their participation in decision-making in schools and neighbourhoods (for methodological and ethical considerations, see Morrow 2000, 2001a, b, 2002; at the time of the research there was no formal research ethics committee at the researcher's institution, and advice and support were provided by an informal advisory group within the local Health Promotion Agency in the county in which the research was conducted).

The next section describes obtaining informed consent, reporting back to children their views on being involved in the research, and presents an ethical dilemma from Project 1.

Seeking informed consent

The challenge of obtaining informed consent from children to participate in research is (somewhat surprisingly) a relatively new issue for social researchers (Alderson 1996; Morrow and Richards 1996). Many researchers have noted the careful negotiations into which researchers enter into in order to carry out research with children. These involve asking adult gatekeepers, particularly in school-based research, where consent is obtained from a series of adults before one can embark on obtaining it from children themselves (James 1993; Prendergast 1994; Mayall 1996). In both projects, each school dealt with the consent process differently, and because head teachers are technically *in loco parentis*, the researcher is guided by them.

In Project 1, in every school, a letter was provided for parents about the project, outlining their option to include or withdraw their child. In the Town schools, the letter was provided in English and Urdu with a covering letter from the head, and in the Town junior school a signed form was returned for children to participate. In Project 2, in School 1, permission was obtained from the head and deputy head teacher and the class teachers in each school to work with whole classes of children. The directors of the Local Education Authority, and the local Health Authority, were informed about the research, and meetings were held regularly with a group that consisted of local health promotion specialists, public health professionals, and representatives of the Planning Dept and Youth and Community Development team in the town council. In School 2, parents/carers were informed that the research was being carried out and were invited to withdraw their child if they wanted to (none were withdrawn). In School 1 the Year 10 sample consisted of a sociology class, and the school felt the students could learn something from being involved in research.

In Project 2, for example, initially children were given a leaflet explaining that the research aimed to explore 'how young people feel about their friends, family and where they live, because (for adults) this may affect their health and well-being'. I was careful not to raise expectations about what the research might produce in the way of change in their environment. This was a point on which staff and students challenged me on several occasions. In the following sessions, children were divided into discussion groups, conducted in adjacent classrooms. These were audio-taped and transcribed. One girl declined to speak, and wrote her responses instead.

In Project 1, consent was sought from the children themselves in the following way. I began by introducing myself and talked about the research. I explained that by working with me, they would be helping me to find out children's opinions and views. This would be written into a report that would hopefully be useful to people working with children in circumstances where children's views needed to be sought. In both projects, I described the tasks I would ask them to do (and when). I asked them for their consent, and talked about confidentiality, anonymity, and privacy – how I phrased this depended on the age of the children. For example, I explained that they were doing the tasks for me: I would be the only person who would see all their work, though if they agreed, bits of what they said/wrote/drew would be used in the report. I told them that what they wrote/said/drew would be confidential to me, though I had a responsibility to help if they told me they had some kind of problem. They also chose their own pseudonyms on the last visit (usually a source of great hilarity, and a useful closure device) and I informed them that the name of the town or village would be disguised in the report. Copies of drawings, photographs, and written work were returned, if the children wanted them, and when time allowed, the groups heard some of the tapes of the discussions played back.

On each visit, I asked: 'Is this OK? Are you happy to do this? If you'd rather not do [task], we can ask [teacher] for a different task, or you can do something else', and I concluded by telling them that at the end of term, I would return to the school and present to them my initial analysis of what they had produced. At the end of the projects, a copy of the final report was sent to each school.

Is this really informed consent?

In all school-based research, there is an uneasy sense that because the research takes place in school, because they have taken letters home, and because their schools, teachers and parents have agreed, they are a 'captive sample'. To this extent, and because children are the 'objects' of schooling, it is possible to argue that they are similarly the 'objects' of the research. As other researchers have suggested, 'the voluntary nature of any student participation in a school-based study may be doubted at a general level' (Wallace *et al.* 1994: 177). Children responded with varying degrees of enthusiasm to tasks, and some topics engaged the children more than others, and this varied between groups and with different ages. In the group discussions some groups discussed volubly and fully, while with others the group dynamic hardly developed at all.

My impression is that if children in a whole-class situation are asked for their consent they all tend to say yes, but a minority of them will simply not participate at all, will write minimally, and/or say virtually nothing in discussion. However, they all wrote, drew or said *something*, even if they did not necessarily speak. In a sense, then, the group method enables a kind of 'informed dissent'. While I took care to ensure they all had a chance to speak, some may have been too shy, and if they chose not to I respected that and did not pressurize them.

There are many issues to consider when doing research in a school setting. First, there is the possibility that the children see the tasks as some kind of test, so I emphasized that it was their opinions and ideas that I was interested in, that there are no right or wrong answers to the questions. Second, discussions may raise issues that the children have never considered or articulated before, and which may always veer towards the highly personal and unsettling. It was useful to have a range of tasks to move on to if a child became upset, as happened on one occasion, when a 9-year-old boy cried as he drew his pet animals who had died (discussed below).

Children's views on being involved in research

The final question I asked the groups in Project 1 was how it had felt being involved in research, and how best they liked to express themselves. This elicited a range of responses, all positive (on reflection, they probably would not have made negative remarks to my face and it would have been better to ask for confidential written feedback; see Edwards and Alldred

1999). Comments included: 'it depends what you're doing it about'; 'it depends who you're talking with, as well'; 'it's often easier to say things than write them down'. One boy said: 'it's cool, you're better than a teacher, cos you can't give us detention and things, can you?! so we can talk to you without feeling pressure, of getting told off, without feeling pressurized'. One girl commented: 'If you were a teacher, I think it would be harder to talk to you, I don't know, because you see them around school everyday.' Some girls described how they felt more comfortable if they shared their experiences – one girl said 'I like a group, so that we can all put in our ideas', and another said 'one-to-one its just us, [in a group] we don't think it's just one of us that's got the problems, it's all of us'. Another girl said: 'so you can think, oh, its not just me...'. In a group of boys, one boy said 'I'd rather write if it was someone I don't know'; and another said 'the only problem with writing is that people can ignore it, and they can just, like, put it aside'. Younger children said they preferred to be with their friends when talking to a researcher.

Reporting back to children

In both projects, I carried out a preliminary general analysis of data, and returned to report back to children at the end of term, mindful that children are dispersed at the end of the school year. Children responded in different ways. On two occasions I was given a round of applause, together with a hail of requests to 'see the report'. In the case of the town 8-year-olds, the children listened to me and asked a few questions about words they did not understand, and in the case of the 10-year-olds, the children asked some highly pertinent questions, such as 'why did you choose us to work with?' and 'who will read the report?'. They asked when I would return to visit them, and this raises the difficult (and rarely discussed) issue of how researchers close the relationship they have developed with the children they are working with.

In Project 2, reporting back proved to be invaluable, because when presenting my preliminary 'findings' to one group, a young man pointed out that I had not mentioned the quality of relationships between students and staff, and that these were extremely important to children's well-being. As a result of his intervention, I refocused the analysis around this topic.

The researcher's role

Educational researchers have distinguished between two roles for researchers, as 'observers' and as 'participants' (Wallace *et al.* 1994). The role of the researcher may be influenced by the age, gender, ethnic background and personal style of the researcher, as well as any previous experience that children may have had of being involved in research. Broadly speaking, the following come to mind: someone to confide in, or a source of advice (particularly for girls); an authority-figure/teacher, to be tested (especially for boys): would I allow them to chew gum in the discussions? would I allow them to wear hats? (both of which were against the school rules); an interesting and sometimes entertaining diversion from the school routine; as a person in my own right: often children asked me about my family circumstances, my children, or what my answers to the questions would be (I always volunteered the information they asked for).

On two occasions in Project 1, girls in primary schools went to some lengths to ask my advice. I wondered whether some children saw me as a 'mother figure'. This highlights how children do not necessarily have ready access to objective, unconnected adults in the regular course of events. Children are always in a structural relationship to adults around them: as a child of their families, as somebody's son or daughter, or a 'school' child. School children are in a particular 'working' relationship with teachers, and this relationship may be purely 'professional', as one teacher described it. Moreover, there is often simply not time for teachers and children to talk on a one-to-one basis. Gender, of both the researcher and the children, is likely to be crucial here: had I been a male researcher, would boys have seen me as 'someone to talk to'? Gender may be a factor in 'wanting to talk' and this may affect the research process, especially when 'talking' is the main method of data collection.

What happens when things go wrong?

I turn now to a brief description of an example of 'when things went wrong'. In Project 1, a 9-year-old boy, Sam, began to cry when he started work on his drawing of 'who's important' – he drew who he missed, his dad and his pet animals. The other children (all girls) who were sitting at the same table explained to me very calmly and matter-of-factly that 'he always gets upset when he thinks about his animals'. I asked Sam if he wanted to carry on with his drawing, or wanted to go back to his teacher but he insisted on staying, so I asked him to try to think about his future family – and he drew a fantasy picture of his mum, sister and himself with some tropical animals. He became very absorbed in doing this, and with one other boy was the last to finish. He explained (when most of the other children had gone back to their class), that he had drawn his dad and dead animals because he missed them, and this had made him feel sad: he explained 'I miss my dad, because he's working away – he only comes back at weekends, he's working [a long way from home]'. He and the other remaining boy, Richard, chatted briefly to each other. Richard said:

'Animals do die, that's the trouble ...'. Sam replied: 'But then so do we ...'. I commented to their teacher that Sam had become upset, and mentioned how I had distracted him. She told me about a song they sing regularly in school about the future of wildlife and this possibly explains Sam's association of exotic animals with the future. When I returned the following week to do group discussions, Sam and a girl asked if they could take my tape recorder into a corner of the room and record their own 'interview'. This again involved Sam talking (but without crying this time) about his pets. As a researcher, however, I felt that I had trespassed into Sam's emotional world quite wrongly (especially when Sam mentioned that he missed his dad, I imagined something much worse than his father working away from home) – but this does beg the question of whether or not it is 'OK' to cry. In this case I had 'breached confidentiality' and mentioned my concern to the teacher (who was familiar with Sam's pets' deaths). However, I was left with an awkward sense that the mantra that researchers repeat about confidentiality when obtaining 'informed consent' with children ('what you write/say/draw/photograph will be confidential to the researcher, but if you disclose something that worries me I have a responsibility to help, but I'll discuss it with you first') is inadequate and the reality of research is much more complex.

Implications for ethical research with children

My experience in research with children is that it is difficult, if not impossible, to predict what kind of ethical dilemma is likely to arise. The following may be helpful suggestions:

- Read as widely as possible – ethics guidelines as well as researchers' accounts.
- Discuss issues with colleagues, and try to anticipate how one might respond to a dilemma.
- Ensure that sound back-up, in the form of a research team or an advisory group, is provided.
- Consider assumptions – in the UK the assumption that preoccupies researchers is that children are likely to disclose some form of physical or sexual abuse, but this relates to the points made above about children's perceived vulnerability and their position as 'victims'; in my experience there are many other ethical dilemmas that arise.

There has been a rapid and welcome rise in research, consulting with and listening to children that is very welcome. However, there is also an increasing awareness – and perhaps impatience – that research is not bringing about much change (Donnelly 2003). We now have a clear, well-researched picture of what matters to children, and it makes sense to build upon what has been done, not least because there may be a danger of 'consultation overload' or 'burn-out' – asking children similar questions, repeatedly, without any sign of change, sends negative messages to them about research and its effectiveness. The next stage for childhood research is to explore how (adult) institutions, organizations and structures can take account of research findings based on children's perspectives. There is overwhelming evidence from many sources, participatory projects, research reports, evaluations, audits, and so on, that children are responsive, creative and measured in responding to calls for their views. In an earlier paper, I suggested that incorporating the study of children into social research raises ethical challenges, to which there are no easy solutions. However, to avoid asking the questions because they are ethically difficult, thereby excluding children from research, is an ethical position in itself (Morrow and Richards 1996). My conclusion nearly a decade later is that the biggest ethical challenge now is not only to get adults to listen, but to act upon what they hear.

Summary

In conclusion, the past ten years have seen welcome changes in research with children, and welcome attention to research ethics in general. This chapter has described two research projects and reflected on issues of access, explored the extent to which school-based research can really enable children to consent to research, looked at the researcher's role in school, and described a scenario that raised ethical issues. I have also raised the question of future possibilities for research ethics relating to children and young people.

Further reading

For further information on ethics and research with children, see Alderson and Morrow (2004).

Questions for reflection

1 What are the main differences between children and adults in research in terms of research ethics?
2 How does a researcher's standpoint affect the way he/she sees children and what are the consequences of this for thinking about ethical issues?

3   Schools provide a convenient setting for conducting research with children. What ethical issues need to be considered in school research?

References

Alderson, P. (1993) *Children's Consent to Surgery*. Buckingham: Open University Press.

Alderson, P. (1995) *Listening to Children: Children, Ethics and Social Research*. London: Barnardo's.

Alderson, P. (1996) *Young Children's Rights. Exploring Beliefs, Principles and Practice*. London: Jessica Kingsley.

Alderson, P. (2000) Children as researchers, in P. Christensen and A. James (eds) *Research with Children. Perspectives and Practices* (pp. 241–57). London: RoutledgeFalmer.

Alderson, P. and Morrow, V. (2004) *Ethics, Social Research and Consulting with Children and Young People*. Barkingside: Barnardo's. Updated version of Alderson (1995).

Boyden, J. and Ennew, J. (1997) *Children in Research: A Manual for Participatory Research with Children*. Stockholm: Radda Barnen.

Brannen, J. and O'Brien, M. (1996) *Children in Families: Research and Policy*. London: Falmer Press.

Butler, I. and Williamson, H. (1994) *Children Speak: Children, Trauma and Social Work*. Harlow: NSPCC/Longman.

Donnelly, E. (2003) *Consulting Children and Young People in Liverpool*. Liverpool: Liverpool City Council.

Edwards, R. and Alldred, P. (1999) Children and young people's views of social research: The case of research on home–school relations, *Childhood*, 6(1): 261–81.

Ennew, J. (1994) *Childhood as a Social Phenomenon: National Report, England and Wales*. Vienna: European Centre for Social Welfare Policy and Research.

Fine, G.A. and Sandstrom, K.L. (1988) *Knowing Children: Participant Observation with Minors*. Newbury Park, CA: Sage Publications.

Grodin, M. and Glantz, L. (eds) (1994) *Children as Research Subjects: Science, Ethics and Law*. New York: Oxford University Press.

Her Majesty's Stationery Office (HMSO) (1989) *Children Act 1989*. London: Queen's Printer of Acts of Parliament.

International Year of the Family (1994) *Agenda for Action*. http://www.iyfanniversary.org/states.html#1

James, A. (1993) *Childhood Identities: Self and Social Relationships in the Experience of the Child*. Edinburgh: Edinburgh University Press.

James, A., Jenks, C. and Prout, A. (1998) *Theorising Childhood*. Cambridge: Polity Press.

Johnson, V., Hill, J. and Ivan-Smith, E. (1995) *Listening to Smaller Voices: Children in an Environment of Change*. London: Actionaid.

Kellett, M., Forrest, R. (age 10), Dent, N. (age 10) and Ward, S. (age 10) (2004) 'Just teach us the skills please, we'll do the rest': Empowering ten-year-olds as active researchers, *Children & Society*, 18(5): 329–43.

Lansdown, G. (1994) Children's rights, in B. Mayall (ed.) *Children's Childhoods. Observed and Experienced* (pp. 33–44). London: Falmer Press.

Mayall, B. (ed.) (1994) *Children's Childhoods: Observed and Experienced*. London: Falmer Press.

Mayall, B. (1996) *Children, Health and the Social Order*. Buckingham: Open University Press.

Mayall, B. (2002) *Towards a Sociology for Childhood. Thinking from Children's Lives*. Buckingham: Open University Press.

Morrow, V. (1998a) *Understanding Families: Children's Perspective*. London: National Children's Bureau/Joseph Rowntree Foundation.

Morrow, V. (1998b) 'If you were a teacher, it would be harder to talk to you': Reflections on qualitative research with children in school. *International Journal of Social Research Methodology: Theory and Practice*, 1(4): 297–313.

Morrow, V. (1999a) 'We are people too': Children's perspectives on rights and decision-making in England. *International Journal of Children's Rights*, 7: 149–70.

Morrow, V. (1999b) Conceptualising social capital in relation to the well-being of children and young people: a critical review, *Sociological Review*, 47(4): 744–65.

Morrow, V. (2000) 'Dirty looks' and 'trampy places' in young people's accounts of community and neighbourhood: implications for health inequalities, *Critical Public Health* (Special Issue on Health Inequalities), 10: 141–52.

Morrow, V. (2001a) *Networks and Neighbourhoods: Children's and Young People's Perspectives*. London: Health Development Agency. http://www.hda-online.org.uk/downloads/pdfs/netneigh.pdf

Morrow, V. (2001b) Using qualitative methods to elicit young people's perspectives on their environments: Some ideas for community health initiatives, *Health Education Research: Theory and Practice*, 16(3): 255–68.

Morrow, V. (2002) Children's rights to public space: Environment and curfews, in B. Franklin (ed.) *The New Handbook of Children's Rights: Comparative Policy and Practice*. London: Routledge.

Morrow, V. and Richards, M.P. (1996) The ethics of social research with children: An overview, *Children & Society*, 10: 90–105.

Nicholson, R. (ed.) (1986) *Medical Research with Children: Ethics, Law and Practice*. Oxford: Oxford University Press.

Prendergast, S. (1994) *'This is the Time to Grow Up': Girls' Experiences of Menstruation in School*, 2nd edn. London: Family Planning Association.

Putnam, R. (1993) *Making Democracy Work*. Princeton, NJ: Princeton University Press.

Qvortrup, J. (1987) The sociology of childhood. Introduction. Reprinted from 'The Sociology of Childhood', (ed.) J. Qvortrup, *International Journal of Sociology*, 17(3): 3–37.

Ruddock, J. and Flutter, J. (2004) *How to Improve Your School*. London and New York: Continuum.

Smart, C., Neale, B. and Wade, A. (2001) *The Changing Experience of Childhood: Families and Divorce*. Cambridge: Polity.

Stanley, B. and Sieber, J.E. (1992) *Social Research on Children and Adolescents: Ethical Issues*. Newbury Park, CA: Sage.

United Nations (1991) *United Nations Convention on the Rights of the Child*. New York: United Nations.

Waksler, F. (ed.) (1991) *Studying the Social Worlds of Children: Sociological Readings*. London: Falmer Press.

Wallace, G., Rudduck, J. and Harris, S. (1994) Students' secondary school careers: Research in a climate of moving perspectives, in D. Halpin and B. Troyna (eds) *Researching Education Policy: Ethical and Methodological Issues* (pp. 170–83). London: Falmer Press.

13 New times in ethical research with children
Ann Farrell

Research with children has entered a new era for research ethics and childhood studies (see Jenks 2000; Rotenstreich 2003). Not only has the field of research ethics come to pervade approaches to research with children, but also the field of childhood studies and its attendant understandings of children's competence to engage in research have come to inform its practice.

This era of research with children is emblematic of the new times of globalized productivity (see Gee *et al.* 1996) in areas such as research, on the one hand, and systematic protective surveillance of children, on the other (Farrell 2004). Characteristic of the new global order is the phenomenon of risk and risk management, where risk consciousness undergirds the ethical practice and surveillance of research with children. Danby and Farrell (2004) argue that children are seen to be living in increasingly risky spaces, or, in the nomenclature of Ulrich Beck (2002: 1), in 'risk societies' (see also Mayall 2002; Moss 2002; Moss and Petrie 2002; Farrell 2004). In turn, children's lives, including their participation in research, appear to be governed increasingly by adult policies designed to protect children from perceived harm and danger. Such measures are driven largely by moral concern for the safety of children, in order to shield them from risks posed by adults and other children (Jenks 1996; Walkerdine 1999, 2001; Farrell 2001, 2004; James and James 2001). Ironically, such protective measures may, in fact, curtail the opportunities for children to participate fully in research. In all, these new times challenge practitioner-researchers and research gatekeepers to grapple with the ethical aspects of doing research with children.

Juxtaposed with globalized risk and risk minimization is the research thrust towards transformative research with children and those around them. Just as children's opportunities for participation in research may be declining due to risk management of their lives, so too is there a push towards transformative opportunities that seek to increase their engagement in research. As discussed in Chapter 9, child research offers the potential to transform relations between researchers and those being researched and to produce greater equity and social justice than would otherwise be possible. A major impetus for such transformative work has been the human rights agenda.

Children's rights

In the twentieth century, the children's rights agenda was fuelled by resistance to what was seen as hegemonic racial, ethnic, gender and economic oppression (Firestone 1971; Farson 1974; Holt 1974; Minow 1986; Archard 1993; Farrell 2004). As noted by Farrell (2004), children's rights were taken up in various disciplines, including the social sciences (Franklin 1986, 1995; Bell 1993), the health sciences (Bradley 2000; Milburn 2001; Salek and Edgar 2002; Berg and Latin 2004), philosophy (Archard 1993; Ekman Ladd 1996), legal theory (Freeman and Veerman 1992; Eekelaar 1994; Freeman 1996; Smith 1997) and political science (O'Neill 1995). In the late twentieth century, children's rights were articulated globally in the United Nations Convention on the Rights of the Child 1989 (UNCRC) (Babbie 1998; Kimmel 1988).

Not surprisingly, the decade following the UNCRC saw unprecedented attention to breaches of children's rights. In Australia the *Seen and Heard Report* (Australian Law Reform Commission/Human Rights and Equal Opportunity Commission (ALRC/HREOC) 1997), for example, demonstrated that Australia's legal processes had ignored and mistreated children, and recommended widespread reform to give effect to the rights of children to be both seen and heard. This Australian analysis resonated with Smith's (1997) analysis of judicial ambivalence towards children's rights in England.

While there may be evidence of socio-legal support for children's rights as articulated in the UNCRC, there is still considerable resistance to the notion of children's rights, given that they are seen by some as potentially subversive of parental rights. Lansdown (2001), for example, identifies resistance based on adult concern that children, outside the protective gaze of their parents, may pose a threat to social order (Sutherland 1992; Franklin 1995).

Understandings of children's rights also serve to frame our ethical conduct of research with children. Grodin and Glantz (1994) identify the powerful tension between two sometimes conflicting agendas: protecting children from harm and exploitation in research, on the one hand, and expanding research knowledge of children in order to achieve beneficial outcomes for children and a civil society, on the other.

Undoubtedly, the UNCRC was a watershed in the global articulation of children's rights as human rights. Alderson (2002) argued that the UNCRC opened up human rights as inalienable rights to children, as people in their own right, to whom human dignity should be accorded (see also Alderson 2003; James and James 2004). In due course, children's human rights in research came to converge with their protective rights, that is, their right to participate in research was synonymized with their right to protection in research. The child's right to protection in research was articulated as a human right within the UNCRC (Balke 1992; UNICEF 1990). The term 'person status' was used by Hart and Pavlovic (1991: 345) to describe the construction of children as persons to whom human dignity should be accorded; not as possessions of their parents, nor necessarily as subordinate to adults (Funder 1996). Alanen and Mayall (2001: xii) believe that contemporary 'children are increasingly, though unevenly, constituted as "persons in their own right"'. Farrell (2004) concurs that children's rights came to be seen as their human rights. While not all signatory countries to the UNCRC adopted the convention as part of their law (e.g. Australia), there is evidence that they have taken major legislative initiatives that have taken serious account of the convention (see Farrell 2001, 2004).

Arguments for convergence aside, children's rights as human rights in research are construed, in many research codes of ethics, as advancing the principle of beneficence, that is, the relative benefit of the research versus the risk to the participant. Australia's *National Statement on the Ethical Conduct of Research With Humans* (Australian Health Ethics Committee 2002: 4.1), for example, outlined the principle of beneficence whereby research involving children should only be conducted where:

- the research is important to their health and well being;
- their participation is indispensable to the research;
- the research method is child-appropriate; and
- the research conditions provide for their physical, emotional or psychological safety.

Researchers and research gatekeepers alike need to ask: Whose interests are being served by the research? What are the views of the research stakeholders, that is, the children themselves, those who are seen as the beneficiaries of the research?

Allied to the principle of beneficence is the principle that, for children to benefit from participation in research, they should be *seen and heard* in research. Again, this was an unambiguous recommendation of Australia's *Seen and Heard Report* (1997), which found that Australia's legal processes had ignored, misunderstood and mistreated children involved in those processes (see Rayner 1997). How, then, is the child to be seen and heard in research? How does the researcher know that children want to be seen and heard in research? What makes children visible and audible in research? Who determines their competence to be seen and heard in research?

Winter (2004) and the Department for Education and Skills (2002) articulate the respective professional and ethical obligations of research to provide children with authentic opportunities to have their views heard and considered in respectful ways. Winter advocates optimal opportunities for children to be heard and to make choices in the daily structures, processes and interactions that frame child research: 'If we are truly committed to listening and honouring children's rights, we will find ways to genuinely hear and respond to each child' (Winter 2004: 25). Central to an ethical orientation to research with children is the notion of children as competent persons who are capable of taking creditable roles in research.

In opening up such roles for children to be seen and heard in research, it is timely to recognize also the likely power imbalances that may exist between the researcher and the researched, in most cases, between adult and child. Woodhead and Faulkner (2000: 31) describe this as the possible 'status and power differentials which shape the processes involved in carrying out research *with* children'. For them, respect for children as social actors in the research enterprise places 'new responsibilities on the adult community to structure children's environments, guide their behaviour and enable their social participation in ways consistent with their understanding, interests and ways of communication, especially in the issues that most directly affect their lives' (Woodhead and Faulkner 2000: 31–2).

There is, however, a possible tension here between protecting children in research, on the one hand, and liberating children through research, on the other. Fox Harding's (1996, 1997) work on child protection has been influential in child policy and state–family relations in both the United Kingdom and Australia (ALRC/HREOC 1997). Fox Harding (1997) identifies two polar approaches on a continuum of seven possible positions on state–family relations (see also Farrell 2004). These are: the *authoritarian* approach, where the state takes an interventionist role towards the child in the family; and, at the opposite end of the continuum, the libertarian *laissez-faire* approach, where there is lack of state intervention in the life of the child and family. The authoritarian approach assumes that the state knows what is best for children and provides for them accordingly, while the *laissez-faire* approach assumes that parents know what is best for their child and can provide accordingly.

These perspectives sit alongside those of American medical ethicist, Ross (1998) who critiques the notions of child protection and child liberation. Ross (1998) notes that child liberationists seek to grant children equal rights to adults, while child protectionists seek to protect children on the grounds that children are less powerful, more vulnerable and more needy of protection than adults. But according to Ross (1998) the human rights needed by children may be not the same as those needed by adults. In her view, adults need negative rights, for example, the rights of non-interference, whereas children need both negative rights (such as the right to not be physically, sexually or emotionally abused) and positive rights (such as the right to education and medical care) (see also Bradley 2000). So, too, John Stuart Mill (1972) suggests that rights have corresponding duties or responsibilities and can be positive rights which require actions from others or negative rights which require the individual to be permitted to act in a certain way without unnecessary restrictions imposed by others.

A key argument proposed by those who resist human rights for children is that decisions affecting children are the responsibility of the family and that children's rights, in effect, subordinate parental rights (see Muehlenberg 1994; Myers 1994; Maley 1998). Child liberationists argue that such an approach exacerbates children's vulnerability and powerlessness (see Alderson 2003; Mayall 2003; David *et al.* 2001).

In turn, the hybrid human rights/child protection imperative has come to undergird much of the regulation and governance of research ethics in research with children. The policy corollary is that ethical research with children needs to account, on the one hand, for children's competence as reliable informants and, on the other hand, for their potential vulnerability due to the possible power imbalances between themselves and adults, or indeed between children within the research encounter.

Listening to children in research

In the spirit of the UNCRC, there has been a growing trend to listen to children, in public policy and in research, particularly in the UK (Lindsay 2000; Roberts 2000; Clark *et al.* 2003; Stafford *et al.* 2003) and Australia (ALRC/HREOC 1997). So too, is there an expanding academic literature on consultation with children, spanning a range of scholarly disciplines (Edwards and Alldred 1999; Woodhead and Faulkner 2000; Malone 2003).

The new wave of sociological research with children noted in Chapters 1 and 5 is concerned with listening to children as reliable informants of their own experience (Danby and Baker 1998; Morrow 1999, 2001a, b; Farrell *et al.* 2002; Farrell and Danby 2004). A persistent challenge in such research is to listen to children in ways that both respect their competence and recognize possible power differentials that may be part of the research encounter. David *et al.* (2001: 347), in referring to much school-based research, identify pedagogic approaches that are 'inscribed with differential power relations'. Dahlberg and Moss (2005: 97) theorize a 'pedagogy of listening' in early childhood institutions that are sites for ethical and poltical practice.

Listening to children and recognizing issues of power in practice, moreover, relate to the process of making decisions *with* children, not just *for* them (Roberts 2000; Clark *et al.* 2003). This is particularly so in the process of gaining the child's consent to participate in the research. Consent requires interactive dialogue, negotiation and renegotiation over time (see also Alderson 1995; Morrow and Richards 1996; Morrow 1999). As argued in Chapter 5, it is neither a question of transferring or displacing power from one group or person to another nor of scaling down adult-oriented research to children. Rather, it is a matter of seeing children as competent persons in their own right, persons who should be listened to; and acting on their (un)willingness to be involved in the research. Roberts (2000) argues that listening to children, hearing children, and acting on what children say are three different activities, although they are frequently elided as if they were not: 'Listening to children is central to recognizing and respecting their worth as human beings. Children are not simply objects, either of concern, of research or of a media story' (Roberts 2000: 238). And this is particularly so in sensitive research (see Allotey and Lazroo 2004; Fontes 2004).

At the end of the day, we need researchers and research gatekeepers who will listen to children, hear what they say and act wisely on what they say. Such work has transformative capacity to create space for children's competent participation and just protection in the research enterprise.

Further reading

For a more detailed review of children's competence in educational research, see Danby and Farrell (2004).

Questions for reflection

1 What strategies might researchers employ to listen to children in research?
2 What are the impediments to listening to children in research?
3 How will the researcher act responsibly on what children say in research?

References

Alanen, L. and Mayall, B. (eds) (2001) *Conceptualising Child–Adult Relations*. London: RoutledgeFalmer.

Alderson, P. (2002) Children, healing, suffering and voluntary consent, in G. Bendelow, M. Carpenter, C. Vautier and S. Williams (eds) *Gender Health and Healing. The Public/Private Divide* (pp. 198–211). London: RoutledgeFalmer.

Alderson, P. (1995) *Listening to Children*. London: Butterworths.

Alderson, P. (2003) *Institutional Rights and Rites. A Century of Childhood*. London: Institute of Education, University of London.

Allotey, P. and Lazroo, C. (2004) The moral high ground: Reflections on ethical dilemmas in unethical circumstances. *Monash Bioethics Review*, 23(4): 78–84.

Archard, D. (1993) *Children, Rights and Childhood*. London: Routledge.

Australian Health Ethics Committee (2002) *National Statement on the Ethical Conduct of Research with Humans*. Canberra: AHEC.

Australian Law Reform Commission/Human Rights and Equal Opportunity Commission (1997) *Seen and Heard: Priority for Children in the Legal Process*. Canberra: Australian Government Publishing Service.

Babbie, E. (1998) *The Practice of Social Research*. Belmont, CA: Wadsworth.

Balke, E. (1992) Children's Rights and the World Summit for Children, *International Journal of Early Childhood*, 24(1): 2–6.

Beck, U. (1992) *Risk Society: Towards a New Modernity*. London: Sage.

Bell, V. (1993) Governing childhood: neo-liberalism and the law, *Economy and Society*, 22(3): 592–605.

Berg, K.E. and Latin, R.W. (2004) *Essentials of Research Methods in Health, Physical Education, Exercise Science and Recreation*. Baltimore, MD: Lippincott Williams and Wilkins.

Bradley, P. (2000) Application of ethical theory to rationing in health care in the UK. A move to more explicit principles? in P. Bradley and A. Burls (eds) *Ethics in Public and Community Health* (pp. 3–19). London: Routledge.

Clark, A., McQuail, S. and Moss, P. (2003) *Exploring the Field of Listening to and Consulting with Young Children*. London: DfES.

Dahlberg, G. and Moss, P. (2005) *Ethics and Politics in Early Childhood Education*. London: RoutledgeFalmer.

Danby, S. and Baker, C. (1998) 'What's the problem?' – Restoring social order in the preschool classroom, in I. Hutchby and J. Moran-Ellis (eds) *Children and Social Competence: Arenas of Action* (pp. 157–86). London: Falmer Press.

Danby, S. and Farrell, A. (2004) Accounting for young children's competence in educational research: New perspectives in research ethics, *Australian Educational Researcher*, 31(3): 35–49.

David, M., Edwards, R. and Alldred, P. (2001) Children and school-based research: 'Informed consent' or 'educated consent'? *British Educational Research Journal*, 27(3): 347–65.

Department for Education and Skills (2002) *Birth to Three Matters*. London: DfES Publications.

Edwards, R. and Alldred, P. (1999) Children and young people's views of social research. The case of research on home–school relations, *Childhood*, 6(2): 261–81.

Eekelaar, J. (1994) The interest of the child and the child's wishes: The role of dynamic self-determinism, in P. Alston (ed.) *The Best Interests of the Child. Reconciling Culture and Human Rights* (pp. 42–61). Oxford: Clarendon Press.

Ekman Ladd, R. (1996) *Children's Rights Revisioned: Philosophical Readings*. Belmont, CA: Wadsworth.

Farrell, A. (2001) Legislative responsibility for child protection and human rights in Queensland, *Australia and New Zealand Journal of Law and Education*, 6(1/2): 15–24.

Farrell, A. (2004) Child protection policy perspectives and reform of Australian legislation, *Child Abuse Review*, 13: 234–45.

Farrell, A. and Danby, S. (2004) Methodological insights from children's accounts of everyday practice in school. Paper presented at the Australian Association for Education Research Conference. Melbourne, 28 November – 2 December.

Farrell, A., Tayler, C. and Tennent, L. (2002) Early childhood services: What can children tell us? *Australian Journal of Early Childhood*, 27(3): 12–17.

Farson, R. (1974) *Birthrights*. London: Collier Macmillan.

Firestone, S. (1971) *The Dialectic of Sex. The Case for Feminist Revolution*. London: Jonathan Cape.

Fontes, L.A. (2004) Ethics in violence against women research: The sensitive, the dangerous, and the overlooked. *Ethics and Behavior*, 14: 141–74.

Fox Harding, L.M. (1996) *Family, State and Social Policy*. London: Macmillan.

Fox Harding, L.M. (1997) *Perspectives in Child Care Policy*, 2nd edn. London: Longman.

Franklin, B. (1986) *The Rights of Children*. Oxford: Blackwell.

Franklin, B. (1995) *Handbook of Children's Rights: Comparative Policy and Practice*. London: Routledge.

Freeman, M. (ed.) (1996) *Children's Rights: A Comparative Perspective*. Brookfield, VT: Dartmouth.

Freeman, M. and Veerman, P. (eds) (1992) *The Ideologies of Children's Rights*. London: Martinus Nijhoff.

Funder, K. (1996) *Citizen Child*. Melbourne: Australian Institute of Family Studies.

Gee, J.P., Hull, G. and Lankshear, C. (1996) *The New Work Order. Behind the Language of the New Capitalism*. St Leonards, NSW: Allen & Unwin.

Grodin, M. and Glantz, L. (eds) (1994) *Children as Research Subjects: Science, Ethics and Law*. New York: Oxford University Press.

Hart, S.N. and Pavlovic, Z. (1991) Children's rights in education: An historical perspective, *School Psychology Review*, 20(3): 345–58.

Holt, J. (1974) *Escape from Childhood. The Needs and Rights of Children*. Harmondsworth: Penguin.

James, A.L. and James, A. (2001) Tightening the net: Children community and control, *British Journal of Sociology*, 52(2): 211–28.

James, A.L. and James, A. (2004) *Constructing Childhood. Theory, Policy and Social Practice*. New York: Palgrave Macmillan.

Jenks, C. (1996) *Childhood*. London: Routledge.

Jenks, C. (2000) Zeitgeist research on childhood, in P. Christensen and A. James (eds), *Research with Children. Perspectives and Practices* (pp. 62–76). London: Falmer Press.

Kimmel, A.J. (1988) *Ethics and Values in Applied Social Research.* Beverly Hills, CA: Sage Publications.

Lansdown, G. (2001) Children's welfare and children's rights, in P. Foley, J. Roche and S. Tucker (eds), *Children in Society: Contemporary Theory, Policy and Practice.* London: Palgrave.

Lindsay, G. (2000) Researching children's perspectives: Ethical issues, in A. Lewis and G. Lindsay (eds) *Researching Children's Perspectives* (pp. 3–19). Buckingham: Open University Press.

Maley, B. (1998) Children's Rights Ascendent, *Quadrant*, 42(6): 32–6.

Malone, S. (2003) Ethics at home: Informed consent in your own backyard, *Qualitative Studies in Education*, 16(6): 797–815.

Mayall, B. (2002) *Towards a Sociology for Childhood: Thinking from Children's Lives.* Buckingham: Open University Press.

Mayall, B. (2003) Sociologies of childhood and educational thinking (professorial lecture). London: Institute of Education, University of London.

Milburn, M. (2001) *Informed Choice of Medical Services. Is the Law Just?* Ashgate: Aldershot.

Mill, J.S. (1972) On moral obligation and justice, in H.B. Acton (ed.) *Utilitarianism* (pp. 40–2). London: J.M. Dent.

Minow, M. (1986) A feminist approach to children's rights, *Harvard Women's Law Journal*, 9: 1–24.

Morrow, V. (1999) 'We are people too': Children's and young people's perspectives on children's rights and decision-making in England, *International Journal of Children's Rights*, 7: 149–70.

Morrow, V. (2001a) *Networks and Neighbourhood: Children's and Young People's Perspectives.* London: National Health Service.

Morrow, V. (2001b) Using qualitative methods to elicit young people's perspectives on their environment: Some ideas for community health initiatives, *Health Education Research: Theory and Practice*, 16(3): 255–68.

Morrow, V. and Richards, M. (1996) The ethics of social research with children: An overview, *Children & Society*, 10: 90–105.

Moss, P. (2002) Time to say farewell to 'early childhood?', *Contemporary Issues in Early Childhood*, 3(3): 435–8.

Moss, P. and Petrie, P. (2002) *From Children's Services to Children's Spaces: Public Policy, Children and Childhood.* London: RoutledgeFalmer.

Muehlenberg, B. (1994) *In Defence of the Family.* Melbourne: Australian Family Association.

Myers, J. (1994) *The Blacklash: Child Protection under Fire.* London: Sage.

Roberts, H. (2000) Listening to children: and hearing them, in P.H. Christensen and A. James (eds) *Research with Children: Perspectives and Practices* (pp. 225–40). London: Falmer Press.

Ross, L.F. (1998) *Children, Families and Health Care Decision Making.* Oxford: Oxford University Press.

Rotenstreich, N. (2003) *The Dictionary of the History of Ideas*. Charlottesville, VA: Gale Group.

Salek, S. and Edgar, A. (2002) *Pharmaceutical Ethics*. Chichester: Wiley.

Smith, C. (1997) Children's rights: judicial ambivalence and social resistance, *International Journal of Law, Policy and the Family*, 11: 103–39.

Stafford, A., Laybourn, A., Hill, M. and Walker, M. (2003) 'Having a say': Children and young people talk about consultation, *Children & Society*, 17: 361–73.

Sutherland, E. (1992) The role of children in the making of decisions which affect them, in M. Freedman and P. Veerman (eds) *The Ideologies of Children's Rights*. London: Martinus Nijhoff.

UNICEF (1990) *First Call for Children. World Declaration and Plan of Action from the World Summit for Children*. UNICEF: New York.

Walkerdine, V. (1999) Violent girls and precocious girls: Regulating childhood at the end of the millennium, *Contemporary Issues in Early Childhood*, 1(1): 3–23.

Walkerdine, V. (2001) Safety and danger, in K. Hultquist and G. Dahlberg (eds) *Governing the Child in the New Millennium* (pp. 2–34). London: RoutledgeFalmer.

Winter, P. (2004) Respectful relationships: Listening to the voices of infants and toddlers in care, *Every Child*, 10(2): 24–5.

Woodhead, M. and Faulkner, D. (2000) Subjects, objects or participants? in P. Christensen and A. James (eds) *Research with Children. Perspectives and Practices* (pp. 9–33). London: Falmer Press.

14 New possibilities for ethical research with children
Ann Farrell

New times in research ethics are opening up new possibilities for transforming research with children. These new possibilities come from listening to children in ways that respect them as competent participants and acting on their accounts in a responsible and just way. This includes listening to them and respecting their informed consent to participate as well as their right to decline involvement or to withdraw from research once it is under way. So we need to listen to children, hear what they say and act wisely on what they say. This approach favours the sociology of childhood framework, where children's competent versions of their own lived experience are acknowledged and valued. This stands in contrast to traditional approaches which saw children as not yet ready to consent to and participate in research.

Ethical research needs also to account for the contexts in which the research is produced and the prevailing assumptions about children that pervade those contexts. As Edwards and Alldred (1999: 266) argue:

> It is not just children and young people's competence to consent that is dependent on context and substance, but that context and substance also inform how they understand the research and make decisions about whether or not to participate.

The very process of researchers seeking and establishing access to child participants is circumscribed by the prevailing assumptions about adults' protective responsibilities towards children. Hood *et al.* (1996) argue that the socio-political positioning of children means that adults still often give consent on behalf of their children, sometimes exercising their protective duties at the expense of the child exercising their own right to consent. Adults' duty of care towards children, then, may limit children's opportunities to participate fully in research. Hood *et al.* (1996: 118) argue that 'children constitute a social group, whose interests are not necessarily harmonious with those of "the home" and its adults, and are not necessarily coterminous with the values of the home and the school'. Likewise, Roberts (2000: 225) contends that 'Research agendas are still largely the province of adults and children's accounts tend to be edited, reformulated or truncated to fit our agendas. Listening to children is central to recognizing and respecting their worth as human beings.'

While we may see and hear children as valuable and competent research participants, we also need to recognize the lingering power differentials between children and adults and between children and other children that have come to inscribe much research. Very often human research is intrusive and the researcher penetrates the life space of the child and those around them, sometimes with scant evidence of their permission to do so. Given the capacity of research to intrude, we need to ensure that we account for and respect these spaces. It is not a matter of transferring or displacing power from the powerful to the powerless, or of downsizing or upsizing procedures used with one group so that they can be used with another. Rather, it is a matter of seeing children as *bone fide* research players and decision-makers and ensuring that they are legitimized as such throughout the whole research cycle.

Real-world research can not remove complexity from the research or from the lives of children who engage in research. Rather it acknowledges the reality of children's everyday lives and the spaces in which they provide consent to and engage in the research. 'We must learn to live in the middle of things, in the tension of conflict, confusion and possibility; and we must become adept at making do with the messiness of that condition' (Merriam 2002: 401). Children need to be respected as capable of contributing to the veracity of the research. Worked out in partnership with children and those around them, this approach has the potential benefit of generating multiple perspectives on their experience and providing opportunities for their experience to be transformed. In pursuing transformation, Kincheloe (2003: 24) argues that considering social processes historically 'moves us to uncover the genesis of those assumptions that shape our lives and institutions and to ask how they can be altered'.

These approaches open up new possibilities for us to pursue beneficent research where children themselves can benefit from participation in research in ways that are respectful of their competence and advance their human rights. This requires their equitable access to information about the research and opportunities to communicate openly about the research. Research, then, can open up transforming possibilities for children and those around them. It can contest the assumptions which circumscribe children's lives and can provide authentic opportunities for children to engage as competent participants in research.

References

Edwards, R. and Alldred, P. (1999) Children and young people's views of social research. The case of research on home–school relations, *Childhood*, 6(2): 261–81.

Hood, S., Kelley, P. and Mayall, B. (1996) Children as research subjects: A risky enterprise. *Children & Society*, 10, 117–28.

Kincheloe, J.L. (2003) *Teachers as Researchers. Qualitative Inquiry as a Path to Empowerment*, 2nd edn. London: RoutledgeFalmer.

Merriam, S.B. (ed.) (2002) *Qualitative Research in Practice*. San Francisco: Jossey-Bass.

Roberts, H. (2000) Listening to children: and hearing them, in P. Christensen and A. James (eds) *Research With Children. Perspectives and Practices* (pp. 225–40). London: Falmer Press.

Index